2nd EDITION

KV-512-507

...urgh's English-Speaking Union
...h Language Award 2004
...OMMENDED

Skills in English

English

Level 3

Speaking

Teacher's Book

Terry Phillips

and

Anna Phillips

Garnet
EDUCATION

Published by
Garnet Publishing Ltd.
8 Southern Court
South Street
Reading RG1 4QS, UK

First edition, copyright © 2004 Garnet Publishing Ltd.
Second edition, copyright © 2005 Garnet Publishing Ltd.

The right of Terry Phillips and Anna Phillips to be identified as
the authors of this work has been asserted by them in
accordance with the Copyright, Designs and Patents Act 1988.

All rights reserved.
This work is copyright, but copies may be made of the pages
marked *Photocopiable* without fee or prior permission,
provided that these copies are used solely within the
institution for which the work is purchased. For copyright in
other circumstances, prior permission in writing must be
obtained from Garnet Publishing Ltd.

ISBN 1 85964 795 2

British Library Cataloguing-in-Publication Data
A catalogue record for this book is available from
the British Library.

Production

Project manager:	Richard Peacock
Editorial team:	Lucy Thompson, Nicky Platt
Art director:	David Rose
Design:	Mark Slader
Typesetting:	Samantha Barden
Illustration:	Beehive Illustration (Pete Smith/ Pulsar Studio), Doug Nash, Karen Rose
Photography:	Corbis, Digital Vision, Image Source, Photodisc

Garnet Publishing wishes to thank the following
for their assistance in the development of this project:
Dr Abdullah Al Khanbashi, Abderrazak Ben Hamida,
Maxine Gillway, Susan Boylan and the Level 3 team at UGRU,
UAE University

Every effort has been made to trace the copyright holders
and we apologize in advance for any unintentional
omissions. We will be happy to insert the appropriate
acknowledgements in any subsequent editions.

Audio production: John Green TEFL Tapes

Printed and bound
in Lebanon by International Press

Contents

Book Map

Theme	Speaking tasks	Phonology	Oral skills
1 Education, It's Not My Style	Revision	Revision	• Revision
2 Daily Life, Are You a Maximizer or a Satisficer?	Reporting on reading research	Linking – C + V; V + V	• Stating sources
3 Work and Business, The Person and the Problem	Reporting on case studies	Linking – suppressed plosives	• Talking about importance and relevance
4 Science and Nature, Adapting to the Climate	Classifying animals and talking about adaptations	Shifting word stress – 'hibernate, hiber'nation	• Indicating partial comprehension
5 The Physical World, Do You Know Your Region?	Describing a region		• Using the definite article with proper nouns • Comparing more than two things
6 Culture and Civilization, That's Terrible!	Describing death customs	Making and using question tags	• Giving and reacting to bad news
7 They Made Our World, Liquid Crystals	Describing an invention		• Describing a device
8 Art and Literature, Sindbad the Sailor	Telling a story	Elided and weak form of would	• Talking about events before the time of a story • Presenting problems and solutions
9 Sports and Leisure, Where Shall We Go?	Describing a tourist attraction		• Giving an opinion • Making a suggestion • Being a chairperson
10 Nutrition and Health, More Truths and Myths	Revision	Revision	• Revision

INTRODUCTION

The series

This course is part of the four-level *Skills in English* series. The series as a whole prepares students to study wholly or partly in English medium at tertiary level.

In addition, there is a remedial / false beginner course, *Starting Skills in English*, for students who are not ready to begin Level 1.

At each level there are four courses, each dealing with a discrete skill: Listening, Speaking, Reading or Writing. The focus in a particular course is very definitely on that skill. The methodology notes below repeatedly stress the discrete skills focus, and caution against spending too much time on, for example, Writing in this Speaking Skills course. This is not because the writer dislikes integrated skills. The insistence on the target skill is because the writer believes that some students need one or two skills more than the others, and that students should be allowed to make differential progress in the four skills rather than constantly being held to the level at which they can hear, say, read and write a common set of language items.

In all four skills books, the course is organised into 10 themes, each with particular thematic focus. The 10 themes are:

Theme 1:   Education
Theme 2:   Daily Life
Theme 3:   Work and Business
Theme 4:   Science and Nature
Theme 5:   The Physical World
Theme 6:   Culture and Civilization
Theme 7:   They Made Our World
Theme 8:   Art and Literature
Theme 9:   Sports and Leisure
Theme 10:   Nutrition and Health

If you are using other skills books in the series, we recommend that you use them in the following sequence:

Listening
Speaking
Reading
Writing

The commonality of theme across the four skills means that the more skills books you use, the deeper and wider the student's linguistic ability to communicate in that thematic area becomes.

This course

This is the Speaking Skills course at Level 3. The aim is to introduce students with an upper intermediate level of general English to the skills involved in speaking in class and in tutorial groups.

The course comprises the Student's Book, this Teacher's Book, a CD / cassette containing all the listening material, and a Test Booklet.

The course stands alone – in other words, it is not necessary for students to have studied any of the other Skills courses in order to benefit from this course. However, the uniformity of theme across the level means that students who do study two or more Skills courses from the series can carry forward their knowledge.

The Test Booklet contains one test for each theme, a revision test after Themes 1 to 5 and a final test. The tests are sold in packs of ten, with an answer and marking guide. In addition, when you purchase a pack of ten booklets, you get access to an alternative final test on the skillsinenglish.com website. Methodology notes on administering the tests are provided in the answer and marking guide.

Organisation of the course

Each theme contains four lessons. Each lesson has a clear focus and purpose, as follows:

Lesson	Focus	Purpose and methodology points
1	Vocabulary	To ensure that students understand and can recognise basic vocabulary that will be needed for the theme.
2	Speaking	To practise the speaking skill; this lesson revises the skills taught in previous themes.
3	Learning new skills	To highlight specific speaking skills of three types: **a** segmental features, such as individual phonemes and minimal pairs; **b** general speaking skills, such as giving personal information; **c** specialist speaking skills, such as talking about research.
4	Applying new skills	To apply skills learnt in Lesson 3 to a new speaking task – usually a parallel task to that in Lesson 2.

Vocabulary

As can be seen from the information about the organisation of the course above, the writer is firmly committed to the importance of vocabulary. This is why one lesson out of every four is devoted to vocabulary and why, in addition, the first activity in many of the other three lessons in each theme is a vocabulary revision exercise. In the case of speaking, students must be able to produce a wide range of words in isolation and, even more importantly, in the stream of speech.

In Lesson 1, key vocabulary is printed down the outer margin. The positioning is deliberate. You and the students should be able to flick back and find a thematic set easily.

There are two sets of words in each case:

The red words

These are all from Level 2. The green words from that level (see below) have become the red words for this. In other words, these are key words which it is assumed students have acquired, in addition to the basic Council of Europe Waystage-level words from this theme. Students correctly placed at this level will therefore know all or most of these from previous language learning. If they do not, you will need to supplement the one or two exercises provided. Students are required to manipulate the words in a number of ways, largely to prove that they understand the meaning. Thus, activities require them to discuss questions using the red words, put the red words into lexical sets or make true sentences about themselves, their family, country, etc., using the red words.

The green words

These are high-frequency words from the thematic set that will be required for the speaking tasks in Lessons 2 or 4. It is essential that, by the end of Lesson 1, the students understand the meaning of these words *and* can correctly produce them in a stream of speech, so that they do not cause problems with production in the later lessons.

In Lessons 2, 3 and 4, there are additional words that will almost certainly be new to the students. Some of these require pre-teaching, in which case there are additional vocabulary activities at the start of the relevant lesson. In most cases, however, these new words are defined in the speaking tasks themselves or deducible from context. Clearly, the ability to wait for definitions in a text and work out meaning from spoken context are key speaking skills; therefore, these new items should not be pre-taught. However, once the students have had the opportunity to understand the items in context, it is quite reasonable to focus on the new vocabulary and try to ensure that some, at least, is remembered in the future.

To enable you and the students to keep track of the thematic sets, these are reproduced at the back of this book and the Student's Book. In addition, they are organised alphabetically with their origins (i.e., as a red or green word) retained.

Input language

The aim of a Speaking course must, obviously, be speaking. But speaking about what, and with what linguistic resources? The writer believes strongly in giving students something they will actually want to talk about, with new, relevant resources to speak about it. However, this takes preparation. You may be surprised at times, especially in Lesson 2, to find a lot of listening and relatively little speaking. Consider this to be, in part, a silent period where students absorb other people's ideas and words, ready to produce their own ideas and words in Lessons 3 and 4.

Skills Checks

These are a key feature of the course. In every theme, there is at least one Skills Check box. The naming of this feature is significant. It is assumed that the students will have heard about most, if not all, of the skills points in these boxes – i.e., they are skills *checks* not skills *presentations*. It is the writer's experience that many students who have gone through a modern language course have *heard of* the majority of skills points but cannot make practical use of them. If you feel in a particular case that the students have no idea about the point in question, spend considerably longer on a full presentation.

In most cases, the students are given an activity to do before looking at the Skills Check box. Thus, a test-teach-test approach is used. This is quite deliberate. With this approach, there is a good chance that the students will be sensitised to the particular point before being asked to understand it intellectually. This is likely to be more effective than talking about the point and then asking the students to try to apply it.

Specific activities

Certain types of activity are repeated on several occasions throughout the book. This is because these activities are particularly valuable in language learning.

Communicative activities

There are a great many communicative activities in the course which involve some kind of information gap. In most cases, each student has to read and remember some information which he / she then uses to complete a task in collaboration with a partner or a group. The input texts for these activities are often placed at the back of the Course Book as well as in the Teacher's Book for the particular lesson. It is recommended that you copy these texts and give them out, rather than referring students to the Course Book page, as this will give you greater control of the students, i.e., when they are allowed to look at the information and when they must work from memory.

Crosswords and puzzles

One of the keys to vocabulary learning is repetition. However, the repetition must be active. It is no good if students are simply going through the motions. The course uses crosswords and other kinds of puzzles to bring words back into consciousness through an engaging activity.

Odd one out

The ability to see the connections between linguistic items – and, therefore, the odd one out – is a key indicator of comprehension and even production in the case of sounds. However, it is often easier to see the odd one out than it is to explain why that item is different. This is why reasons are sometimes given. Where they are not, consider writing the reasons on the board, in jumbled order, if you feel your students will struggle without them.

Gap fill

Filling in missing words or phrases in a sentence or a text, or labelling a map or diagram, indicates comprehension of both the missing items and the context in which they correctly fit. It is also a possible focus for speaking itself. It is generally better to provide the missing items to ensure that all the required items are available to all the students. In the case of Lesson 1, the words are usually available in the word list on the right. In other cases, you might prefer to supply the words or phrases on the board.

In addition, you can vary the approach to gap fills by sometimes going through the activity with the whole class, orally, pens down, then setting the same task individually. Gap fills or labelling activities can be photocopied and set as revision at the end of the theme or later, with or without the missing items box.

Two-column activities

This type of activity is generally better than open-ended questions or gap fill with no box of missing items, as it ensures that all the target language is available to the students. However, the activity is only fully effective if the two columns are dealt with in the following way:
1   Ask students to match the two parts from each column.
2   Ask students to cover column 2 and remember these parts from the items in column 1.
3   Ask students to cover column 1 and remember these parts from the items in column 2.
Additional activities are:
•   Students test each other in pairs.
•   Teacher reads out column 1 – students complete with items from column 2, books closed.
•   With books closed, students write as many of the items as they can remember.

Tables and charts

Students are often asked to transfer information into a table by ticking the correct box, or writing notes or single words in the boxes.

This activity is a good way of testing comprehension of points about spoken language, as it does not require much linguistic output from the students at a time when they should be concentrating on comprehension or analysis of form.

Once the table has been completed, it can form the basis of:
1   a checking activity – students compare their tables, and note and discuss differences;
2   a reconstruction activity – students give the information in the table in full in speech.

Error correction

It was once thought that showing students an error reinforced the error – the students would be even more likely to make that error in the future. We now know that recognising errors is a vital part of language learning. Students must be able to recognise errors – principally in their own work – and correct them. For this reason, error recognition and correction activities are occasionally used. Throughout the course, students are encouraged to recognise and correct errors in the spoken language of their partner.

Methodology points

Setting up tasks

The teaching notes for many activities begin with the word 'Set …'

This single word covers a number of vital functions for the teacher, as follows:
1   Refer students to the rubric – or instructions.
2   Check that they understand **what** to do – get one or two students to explain the task in their own words.
3   Tell the students **how** they are to do the task, if this is not clear in the rubric – as individual work, pairwork or in groups.
4   Go through the example if there is one. If not, make it clear what the target output is – full sentences, short answers, notes, etc.
5   Go through one or two of the actual prompts, working with a good student to elicit the required output.

Use of visuals

There is a large amount of visual material in the book. This should be exploited in a number of ways:

1 before an activity, to orientate the students, to get them thinking about the situation or the activity, and to provide an opportunity for a small amount of pre-teaching of vocabulary;
2 during the activity, to remind students of important language;
3 after the activity, to help with related work or to revise the target language.

In cases where small drawings have been provided of key items, if possible make flashcards of the drawings so the words can be revised quickly whenever time allows. If students are being taught in one room, the flashcards can be permanently displayed on the walls once the relevant items have been covered in class.

Pronunciation

The focus of this Speaking course is on a productive skill rather than a receptive one. However, it is important that students can hear all the target items correctly. In addition, it is arguable that you cannot produce a phoneme or a phonemic distinction (e.g., /p/ vs /b/) until you can hear it. In many cases, the lesson notes suggest drilling; even where they don't, consider spending a few minutes on this vital tool to improvement in articulation.

Comparing answers in pairs

This activity is suggested on almost every occasion when the students have completed an activity individually. This provides all students with a chance to give and explain their answers, which is not possible if the teacher immediately goes through the answers with the whole class.

Monitoring

Pairwork and group activities are, of course, an opportunity for the students to produce spoken language. You can further extend the value of these opportunities by providing the students with some language of organisation – things which help them talk about the task while they are doing it. Write some phrases on the board when relevant, e.g., *This one comes first. No, I think it's that one.*

Another benefit of pairwork and group work is that they provide an opportunity for the teacher to check three points:
1 that the students are performing the correct task, in the correct way;
2 that the students understand the language of the task they are performing;
3 the elements that need to be covered again for the benefit of the whole class, and the points that need to be dealt with on an individual basis with particular students.

Feedback

At the end of each activity, there should be a feedback stage. During this stage, the correct answers (or a model answer in the case of freer activities) are given, alternative correct answers (if any) are accepted, and wrong answers are discussed.
Note: If no answers are provided, answers depend on students.

Feedback can be:
a high-speed, whole-class, oral – this method is suitable for cases where short answers with no possible variations are required;
b individual, oral – this method is suitable where answers are longer and / or where variations are possible;
c individual, on to the board – this method is suitable when the teacher will want to look closely at the correct answers to highlight points of interest or confusion.

Remember – learning does not usually take place when a student gets something right. Learning generally takes place after a student has got something wrong, and begins to understand why it is wrong.

Confirmation and correction

Many activities benefit from a learning tension, i.e., a period of time when students are not sure whether something is right or wrong. The advantages of this tension are:

a a chance for all students to become involved in an activity before the correct answers are given;

b a higher level of concentration from students – (tension is quite enjoyable!);

c a greater focus on the item as students wait for the correct answer;

d a greater involvement in the process – students become committed to their answers and want to know if they are right and, if not, why not.

In cases where learning tension of this type is desirable, the detailed teacher's notes say, 'Do not confirm or correct (at this point).'

Highlighting grammar

This course is not organised on a grammatical syllabus and does not focus on grammar specifically. However, there is necessarily a written grammar which underlies all the work. Students must be able to produce accurate sentences before they can hope to produce accurate paragraphs and texts. Of course, this is a necessary but not sufficient pre-condition. In other words, the course recognises that paragraphs are texts and not simply accurate sentences strung together.

Where the expression *Highlight the grammar* or similar is used in the teacher's notes, this means at least the following:

1 focus the student's attention on the grammar point, e.g., *Look at the verb in the first sentence*;

2 write an example of the target grammar on the board;

3 ask a student to read out the sentence / phrase;

4 demonstrate the grammar point in an appropriate way (see below);

5 refer to the board throughout the activity if students are making mistakes.

Ways of dealing with different kinds of grammar point:

- for **word order**, show the order of items in the sentence by numbering them, e.g.,

1	2	3	4
They	often	have	a special party.

- for **paradigms**, show the changes with different persons of the verb.

I	go
He	go **es**

According to recent corpora research, the main tense that appears in academic text is the simple present. This tense alone accounts for the vast majority of sentences. At the other extreme, in one corpus of four million words, there was only one example of the present perfect continuous. This suggests that we should not spend a huge amount of time on verb tenses in an EAP course. Instead, we need to ensure that students can understand and produce compound and complex sentences in the simple present tense. Rather than in verb tenses, difficulty in academic texts often lies in the use of complex noun phrases with a great deal of pre- and post-modification of the head word, and in the use of long subordinate clauses at the start of sentences. For this reason, *Skills in English* first ensures that students can understand and produce basic SVO patterns and then, gradually, can understand and produce expansion of the S and O and combinations of SVO sentences in various ways.

Self-checking

On several occasions during the course, the teacher's notes encourage you to ask the students to check their own work. In the Speaking course, this can be done by referring students to the full tapescript at the end of the course. This is an excellent way to develop the students' recognition and correction of error. Listening obviously happens inside someone's head, and in the end each student has to understand his / her own error or misunderstanding.

Dealing with dialogues

In nearly every Lesson 2 there is a dialogue which contains key functional language, e.g., asking for and giving opinions. In many cases the dialogue can be exploited thus:

1 Students order the dialogue, match questions and responses or fill in the gaps.

2   Students write out the conversation in a clean form in their exercise books. Weak classes can simply copy; stronger classes can attempt to remember, perhaps from prompts on the board.

3   Students practise the dialogue in pairs. Teacher monitors.

4   Students practise again, taking the other role. Teacher monitors.

5   Teacher feeds back to individual students on particular problems or mistakes.

6   Teacher feeds back to the whole class on general problems and, if necessary, repeats stages 3 and 4 above.

7   Teacher invites a few pairs / groups to demonstrate the dialogue – open pairs. With more extrovert classes, they can be encouraged to act it out too.

Role plays

The exploitation of these activities is similar to **Dealing with dialogues** except that the activity is freer – the students have a choice about what they say and in what order. Do a trial run with a good student to demonstrate the activity. Better students will use all the language from the lesson(s), weaker ones will only use a few items. Monitor and encourage them to use more.

Many of the Language and culture notes in this edition are written for students whose first language is Arabic. If you have students from a different language group, check with the skillsinenglish.com website to see if there are relevant notes. We are constantly increasing the range of languages covered.

Lesson 1: Vocabulary

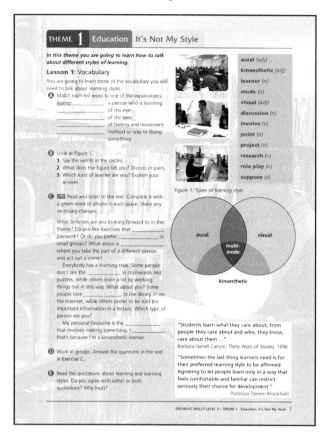

It is assumed that students studying this book have either done Speaking Skills Level 2 of the *Skills in English* course or an equivalent course at that level. In Level 2, students learned how to:

- use signpost words and phrases
- say 'I don't know'
- ask about feelings
- give simple informal advice
- make an arrangement
- compare two things
- express certainty
- apologise
- express an opinion
- talk about information they have heard
- talk about past and present customs
- talk about arrangements
- speak on the telephone
- narrate a story
- explain rules

In addition, they covered the following points of phonology and stress:

- /f/ vs /v/
- diphthongs
- consonant clusters
- sounds of *g*
- regular past tense verbs
- *can* vs *can't* (BrE)
- unstressed function words
- unstressed syllables in words – use of schwa
- stress in multi-syllable words – common patterns:
  - long vowels are often the stressed syllable, e.g., *speaking, argument, important*
  - diphthongs are often the stressed syllable, e.g., *civilization, process, illustration*
  - the vowel before a doubled consonant is often the stressed one, e.g., *marriage, wedding*

Some of these skills are practised in this theme and are assumed knowledge for the rest of Level 3. Note that the aim of this theme is partly to introduce some (more) vocabulary in the lexical set Education, but it is also a norming theme – bringing all students up to the same level in terms of their ability to produce particular sounds and their ability to use certain functional language from Level 2.

If students have done Level 2, the red words (in all themes, not just this one) should be known or at least recognised. Students clearly may have forgotten the meanings, but it should be possible to bring them back relatively easily. If students have not done Level 2, you may have to supplement Exercises A and B with more activities directly presenting the vocabulary as new.

Introduction

Write the subtitle of the theme on the board (*It's Not My Style*). Ask students to guess what it refers to – they should be able to do this easily if they did this theme at Level 2. If not, refer them to the illustrations and elicit the different ways that people are learning – by listening, reading, talking, doing things.

Exercise A

If this is revision, set for individual work then pairwork checking. Otherwise elicit from the whole class.

Answers

learner	a person who is learning
visual	of the eyes
aural	of the ears
kinaesthetic	of feeling and movement
mode	method or way of doing something

Exercise B

Refer students to Figure 1. They will have seen a version of this if they did Level 2. In that case, there was an extra category of learner – *Read/Write*. If students saw the other figure, point out the difference. Explain that some people say there are only three types of learning style plus combinations. If students did not do Level 2, you do not need to mention the difference, but you will need to spend longer on Exercises B1 and B2, below.
1   Drill pronunciation.
2   Set for pairwork. Feed back orally.
3   Elicit ideas.

Language and culture note

Aural is normally pronounced /ɔːrəl/; however, many educationalists pronounce it /aʊrəl/ to distinguish it from /ɔːrəl/ meaning *of the mouth* or *of speech*.

Exercise C

Set for individual work then pairwork checking.

Play the recording. Feed back orally. Check comprehension, perhaps by playing 'stupid teacher',

i.e., reading out the text wrongly for students to correct, e.g., *What **food** are you looking forward to in this theme? Do you like **economics** that involve pairwork? Or do you prefer **disagreements** in small groups? What about a **bread roll**, where you take the part of a different **animal** and **make a scene**?*

*Everybody has a learning **spell**. Some people don't see the point in **crossroads** and puzzles, while others learn a lot by working **out**. What about you? Some people love **searching**, in the library or on the Internet, while others prefer to be told the important information in a **picture**. Which type of person are you?*

*My personal favourite is the project that involves making something. I suppose that's because I'm a **sympathetic** learner.*

Answers
Target words in italics
What activities are you looking forward to in this theme? Do you like exercises that *involve* pairwork? Or do you prefer *discussions* in small groups? What about a *role play*, where you take the part of a different person and act out a scene?

Everybody has a learning style. Some people don't see the *point* in crosswords and puzzles, while others learn a lot by working things *out* in this way. What about you? Some people love *research*, in the library or on the Internet, while others prefer to be told the important information in a lecture. Which type of person are you?

My personal favourite is the *project* that involves making something. I *suppose* that's because I'm a kinaesthetic learner.

Exercise D

Put students into groups. Monitor. Feed back by getting a few students to give their answers.

Exercise E

Students continue in the same groups. Refer them to the first quotation on the right-hand side of the page. Monitor. Refer students to the second quotation. Monitor. Feed back, eliciting some of the best comments.

Closure

Drill the green words. Check particularly the sounds:
- *ssi* (/ʃ/) in *discussion*; point out that the verb is *discuss* with a normal /s/
- the cluster *lv* in *involve*
- the diphthong (/ɔɪ/) in *point*
- the cluster *ct* in *project* and the stress *'project* (therefore no schwa)
- the schwa and the sound of *ear* (/ɜː/) in *research*
- the diphthong (/əʊ/) in *role*
- the schwa and the diphthong (/əʊ/) in *suppose*

Lesson 2: Speaking

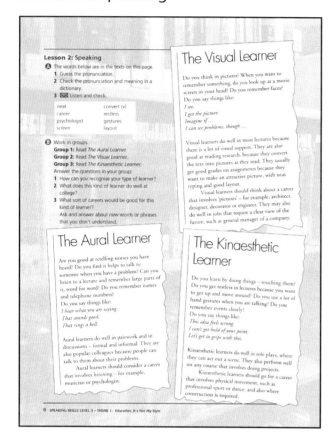

Introduction

If students have done Level 2, they will be familiar with some of the phonemic symbols and will therefore be able to do the second half of Exercise A. If they have not done Level 2, you can:

a   check / teach the target sounds from Exercise A, i.e.,

short vowels: /ɪ/; /ɒ/; /e/; /æ/

long vowels: /iː/; /ɜː/

diphthongs: /ɪə/; /aɪ/; /eɪ/; /aʊ/

problem consonants: s = /s/ or /z/; g = /g/, /dʒ/ or /ŋ/

or

b   leave out Exercise A2.

If you decide to do b above, introduce the lesson by revising the green words from Lesson 1.

Exercise A

1   Do the first word as an example. Point out that the sound is probably /niːt/, from the spelling pattern in *meat*, etc., as *ea* only makes the sound /ɪə/ in front of an *r* (e.g., *ear, fear, rear*). Of course, there are exceptions, e.g., *Earth* (/ɜːθ/) and *wear* (/weə/). Do *career* as a further example.

a   Where is the stress? Remind / tell students that doubled vowels are often stressed syllables in English; therefore, the most likely pattern is *ca'reer*, in which case, …

b   …the first vowel will probably go to schwa – only the letter *i* regularly retains its full value in an unstressed syllable.

c   The letter *c* is normally /k/ in front of the vowel *a*.

d   The doubled *e* could make the sound /iː/, but *eer* is often /ɪə/ as in *engineer, mountaineer*.

So, by a process of deduction, the pronunciation is probably /kə'rɪə/.

Set the rest of the exercise for pairwork. Elicit ideas but do not confirm or correct if you are going to do A2.

2   Give students time to look up the words in their dictionaries. Feed back, writing each word and the phonemic script on the board.

Drill the pronunciation. Point out that the students will have to say some of these words in the next exercise.

Language and culture note

Modern dictionaries, e.g., Collins, give the alternative pronunciation /ɪəl/ for words ending *-eal*, e.g., *ideal*.

Answers

word	phonemics	deduction notes
neat	/niːt/	see above
ca'reer	/kəˈrɪə/	see above
psy'chologist	/saɪˈkɒlədʒɪst/	ps = /s/ y = normally = /aɪ/ in the middle of a word; ch often = /k/ in the middle of a word except after *t*; unstressed short vowels go to schwa except /ɪ/
screen	/skriːn/	only problem here is saying the cluster with no intrusive vowel sounds
con'vert	/kənˈvɜːt/	two-syllable verbs are normally stressed on the second syllable, especially when there is also a noun with the same form; unstressed short vowel goes to schwa; *er* normally = /ɜː/
'restless	/ˈrestlɪs/	this has a suffix which is rarely stressed, therefore first syllable is stressed; stressed *e* = /e/; unstressed goes to /ɪ/
'gestures	/ˈdʒestʃəz/	g = /dʒ/ because it is in front of *e* e = /e/ ture = /tʃə/ as in *lecture, picture*
'layout	/ˈleɪaʊt/	ay = /eɪ/ ou = /aʊ/

Methodology note

The ability to deduce the sound of a word from its spelling (and part of speech) is a key skill. We sometimes tend to say, particularly to beginners, that English is a stupid language when it comes to sound–sight relationships. In fact, the large number of exceptions often hides a common pattern. It is perfectly possible for analytically-minded students to work out the probable sound of a new word like *gesture* by applying these common patterns. It is well worth spending plenty of time pointing out the patterns – as described in the notes to the Answers. Some students will not be able to take them in, but others may well be able to use the information in future.

Exercise B

Put students into groups. Make sure they understand that all the groups must answer the three questions. Elicit some ways of asking about new words – at Level 1 and Level 2 students learned/practised saying:

What does X mean?

Is X a kind of Y?

Does X mean Y?

How do you say this word – X-Y-X [spelling]?

Give plenty of time for this activity. Monitor the groups and ensure that they are working through the text and extracting the answers to the questions.

Feed back with each group, but try not to let the other groups hear the feedback.

Explain that you will give students a chance to work out what kind of learner they are in the next lesson.

Methodology note

Make a record of the membership of each group, as you may want to put students back into these groups in the next lesson.

Closure

Ask students to guess the pronunciation of these unusual words. Point out that they can use the patterns from Exercise A. It doesn't matter about the meaning.

bleat (/bli:t/)

boundless (/ˈbaʊndlɪs/)

defer (v) (/dɪˈfɜː/)

fixture (/ˈfɪkstʃə/)

flay (/fleɪ/)

gel (/dʒel/)

orienteer (/ɔːrɪənˈtɪə/)

psychiatrist (/saɪˈkaɪətrɪst/)

screed (/skri:d/)

Lesson 3: Checking skills

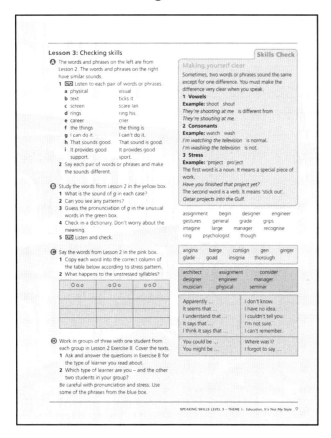

oo	/uː/
ai	/eɪ/
o...e	/əʊ/
ou	/aʊ/

Refer students to the Skills Check. Work through the various points.

Exercise A

1   Point out that students just have to listen to the recording and try to hear the key differences. Highlight the key differences between each pair.
2   Set for pairwork. Monitor and assist.

Exercise B

Refer students to the yellow box. If students studied sounds of the letter *g* at Level 2, use this as revision. Otherwise, point out that the letter *g* makes three main sounds:

/g/   *good; got*
/dʒ/   *message,*
/ŋ/   *wrong, speaking*

1 and 2 Set for pairwork. Feed back onto the board.
3   Point out that the students should now be able to guess the pronunciation from the patterns. Explain that the meanings are not important. Point out that unless you can pronounce a new word it is sometimes difficult to ask someone for the meaning.
4   Set for individual work then pairwork checking. Once again, meaning is not important, although students may of course want to know.
5   Play the recording for students to check their ideas.

Introduction

Remind students of the work in the previous lesson on different types of learner. Explain that you are going to look at pronunciation of particular sounds first, then return to the texts from Lesson 2.

Remind students of the most common sound–sight relationships with vowels:

Letter	Common sound
a	/æ/
e	/e/
i	/ɪ/
o	/ɒ/
u	/ʌ/
i...e	/aɪ/
oi	/ɔɪ/
ar	/ɑː/
er	/ɜː/
ee	/iː/
or	/ɔː/

Answers

There are no rules, but there are some patterns.

pattern	common sound	examples in green box
g + a / o / u	/g/	goad
g + e / i	/dʒ/	gen, ginger
g + l / r	/g/	glade, grips
g + h	silent	thorough
g + n	/g/	signal
	sometimes silent	design
n + g	/ŋ/ at end of word	ring
	/ŋ/ in the middle	ringing, singer
	/g/ or /dʒ/ in the middle	finger, ginger

Of course there are exceptions (e.g., get, forget).

Tell students to check new words in a dictionary if they are not sure.

Exercise C

Do the first couple of words in the pink box as examples.

Set for pairwork. Feed back by building up the table on the board.

Answers

O o o	o O o	o o O
architect	assignment	engineer
manager	consider	
physical	designer	
seminar	musician	

Notes to answers

architect	no schwas – /ɪ/ and /e/ retain full (or almost full) value
assignment	schwa at beginning and end
consider	schwa at beginning and end
designer	/ɪ/ at beginning retains full value, schwa at end
engineer	/e/ and /ɪ/ retain full (or almost full) value
manager	two schwas
musician	/juː/ retains full value; schwa at end
physical	some people say two schwas, others keep /ɪ/
seminar	some people say /ɪ/ in the middle, others schwa; /ɑː/ at the end

Exercise D

Remind students about the texts from Lesson 2. If there has been quite a long gap between that lesson and this, you might want to put students back into the same groups again to revise the work on each of the three texts independently before making the new groups.

Then put students into the required groups of three, with one representative from each group. Get students to cover the text. Ideally, write the questions from Lesson 2 Exercise B on the board so students can close their books. The questions are:

1 *How can you recognise your type of learner?*
2 *What does this kind of learner do well at college?*
3 *What sort of careers would be good for this kind of learner?*

Show how students can record information in a table:

	aural	visual	kinaesthetic
how to recognise			
do well at college?			
careers			

1 Demonstrate how students have to exchange information, e.g., one of the students asks the first question and the other two students answer, then he / she gives information for his / her type of learner. Tell students to be especially careful with pronunciation during this exercise. Point out that they can also use the phrases in the blue box. (See Methodology note.) Monitor and assist, correcting the pronunciation of individual students as you go.

2 When you feel most of the information has been transferred – check students' tables – refer them to the second question of this exercise. Basically, they have to work out from the information they have shared what type of learner they are. Remind them that they could be a combination of types, including all three.

Methodology note

The phrases in the blue box are all from Level 2. If students did this level, just remind them of the usage of these phrases. Clearly, some are about reporting information you have heard or read, some are saying you don't know or are not sure, some are for stating possibilities and some are useful if you get lost / want to backtrack. If students didn't do Level 2, you will need to spend more time explaining and then drilling the phrases.

Closure

Feed back, eliciting ideas from a number of different students.

Lesson 4: Applying skills

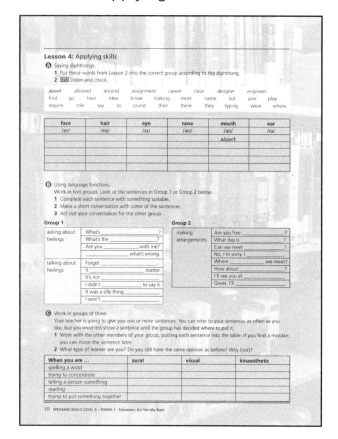

c   Get individual students to say a word – the other students must say the correct number.

Explain that in this lesson the students are going to practise diphthongs (vowels with two sounds).

Exercise A

Show how to complete the table with the example (*about*). Set for individual work then pairwork checking. Feed back, building up the table on the board. Point out common spelling patterns, e.g., *ay* and *a...e* = /eɪ/.

Drill each group of words. Ask students to suggest other words they know with each diphthong.

Answers

face	hair	eye	nose	mouth	ear
/eɪ/	/eə/	/aɪ/	/əʊ/	/aʊ/	/ɪə/
making	*pair*	*assignment*	*go*	*about*	*career*
name	*their*	*designer*	*know*	*allowed*	*clear*
play	*there*	*find*	*most*	*around*	*engineer*
say	*wear*	*require*	*role*	*out*	*hear*
they	*where*	*typing*	*so*	*sound*	*idea*

Exercise B

Remind students who did Level 2 (or tell students who didn't) that there are certain important language functions for students, including *asking about feelings*, *talking about feelings* and *making arrangements*. Write these three 'titles' on the board, side by side. Give an example of each, e.g., *What's wrong? / Forget it. / Are you free now?*

Elicit some more exponents of each function, books closed. Build up a list under each title. Drill for pronunciation and intonation. Work on pitch range, especially for asking and talking about feelings.

Introduction

Remind students of the simple vowels – short and long – from the previous lesson.

Go quickly through the most common sounds, perhaps by getting students to work with these words:

1   pat
2   pet
3   pit
4   pot
5   putt
6   put
7   part
8   pert
9   peat / Pete
10   port

a   Say a word and get students to say the number.
b   Say a number and get students to say the word, chorally then individually.

Erase all the exponents, just leaving the titles.

1   Put students into two groups, or several groups for each set of exponents if you have a large class. Refer students to the relevant list in their books. Set for group work. Go round to the groups and check that they have completed the exponents in suitable ways.

2   Demonstrate how you can use the exponents to make a short conversation. Set for group work. Monitor and assist. Students can write the conversation if they want to.

3   Encourage the groups to act out their conversations.

Feed back on general points.

If you wish and there is time, swap the groups so each gets a chance to do both sets of exponents, and repeat B1–3 above.

Answers

Group 1

asking about feelings
What's *wrong*?
What's the *matter*?
Are you *angry* with me?
Tell me what's wrong.

talking about feelings
Forget *it*.
It *doesn't* matter.
It's not *important*.
I didn't *mean* to say it.
It was a silly thing *to say*.
I won't *do it again*.

Group 2

making arrangements
Are you free *next week*?
What day is *good for you*?
Can we meet *[on Monday at 3 o'clock]*?
No, I'm sorry. I *can't make it then*.
Where *shall* we meet?
How about *[the college cafe]*?
I'll see you at … *on* … *in* ….
Great. I'll *look forward to it*.

Exercise C

Remind students of aural, visual and kinaesthetic learners. Elicit some information about them. Explain that the students are now going to use their knowledge about these different types of learner to complete a puzzle.

1   There are several different ways to conduct this task. They are listed below in order of difficulty – the easiest first. In all cases, the activity is much better if the students actually have a board onto which they can put their sentences.

The two boards are available as photocopiable materials on pages 27 and 28 of this book. Obviously you will need to cut up the sentences into individual cells.

Alternative methods

a   Give out the sentences in groups of three in random order, e.g., first, the three sentences related to *reading*, then the three related to putting something together, etc. Students have to identify which task the sentences relate to and then put them in the correct column.

b   Give out all the 'aural' sentences to one student, all the 'visual' to another and all the 'kinaesthetic' to the third. Students have to identify which group they have first, then decide which section each sentence goes in.

c   Shuffle the sentences and divide into three groups. Give one group to each student – therefore, each student has some from each type of learner. Students have to identify the type of learner and the correct section for each sentence.

In case students get stuck, you might wish to have an OHT version of the solution. You can then display all or part of it at any time to get the students back on track. An OHT version is also the best way to feed back at the end – see overleaf.

2   When a group has got a reasonable answer, move
    them on to the second part of the activity (deciding
    which type of learner they are).

Feed back, ideally with an OHT of the solution.

Answers
Model answer

When you are ...	aural	visual	kinaesthetic
spelling a word	you say the word aloud.	you try to see the word in your mind's eye.	you write the word down.
trying to concentrate	you get disturbed by sounds or noise.	you hate untidiness in your room or on your desk.	you become distracted by activity around you.
telling a person something	you prefer talking on the telephone.	you prefer face-to-face meetings.	you like doing things while you are talking.
reading	you like the parts of stories with conversation and hear it in your head.	you like descriptive scenes in stories. You imagine the places.	you love action stories.
trying to put something together	you need to talk to someone about it.	you need a demonstration or pictures.	you just start trying things straight away – even if there are pictures.

Closure

Feed back, eliciting comments from different students
about the type of learner they think they are from the
information in the table.

When you are …	aural	visual	kinaesthetic
spelling a word	you say the word aloud.	you try to see the word in your mind's eye.	you write the word down.
trying to concentrate	you get disturbed by sounds or noise.	you hate untidiness in your room or on your desk.	you become distracted by activity around you.
telling a person something	you prefer talking on the telephone.	you prefer face-to-face meetings.	you like doing things while you are talking.
reading	you like the parts of stories with conversation and hear it in your head.	you like descriptive scenes in stories. You imagine the places.	you love action stories.
trying to put something together	you need to talk to someone about it.	you need a demonstration or pictures.	you just start trying things straight away – even if there are pictures.

When you are …	aural	visual	kinaesthetic
spelling a word			
trying to concentrate			
telling a person something			
reading			
trying to put something together			

Lesson 1: Vocabulary

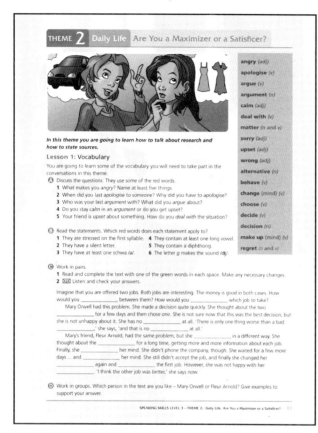

Introduction

If possible, pick on someone who looks worried and ask 'What's wrong? What's the matter?' See if you can elicit an answer. This is further revision for students who did Level 2, or a reminder of the activity in Theme 1 of this level. Elicit how you can reply, putting off the query – *It's OK. It's nothing. I'm all right* or introducing the problem – *It's (my / your / the) …* Use this language throughout this lesson and the whole theme to give students a chance to practise hearing and responding to it.

Exercise A

Set for pairwork. Refer students to the red words. Monitor, making notes of interesting points. Feed back orally, eliciting the interesting points from different pairs.

Exercise B

Drill the pronunciation of the red words. Set for individual work then pairwork checking. Feed back, building up the table on the board. Drill the words again in each group. Then get students to close their books and tell you what each group of words has in common, i.e., tell you again the statements in Exercise B.

Answers

1   *angry, argue, argument, matter, sorry*
2   *calm, wrong*
3   *apologise, argument, matter*
4   *angry, argue, argument, calm, sorry*
5   *apologise, deal*
6   *apologise*

Exercise C

Refer students to the green words. Encourage them to think about the pronunciation but do not confirm or correct – they are going to hear the words later.

1   Set for pairwork. Monitor but do not assist. Make a note of any points that prove particularly difficult.
2   Play the recording. Feed back, ideally onto an OHT of the text. Check the pronunciation of the green words, especially the following points:

alternative	stress, schwa
behave	stress, first e = /ɪ/
change	diphthong (/eɪ/)
choose	long vowel; s = /z/
chose	diphthong (/əʊ/); s = /z/
decide	stress, c = /s/ ; diphthong (/aɪ/)
decision	stress, c = /s/ ; si = /ʒ/
mind	diphthong (/aɪ/)
regret	stress, first e = /ɪ/

Check comprehension of the text with high-speed questions, e.g.,

- *What problem did both Mary and Fleur have?*
- *What did Mary do?*
- *What about Fleur?*

Answers

Target words in italics

Imagine that you are offered two jobs. Both jobs are interesting. The money is good in both cases. How would you *choose* between them? How would you *decide* which job to take?

Mary Orwell had this problem. She made a decision quite quickly. She thought about the two *alternatives* for a few days and then chose one. She is not sure now that this was the best decision, but she is not unhappy about it. She has no *regrets* at all. 'There is only one thing worse than a bad *decision*,' she says, 'and that is no *decision* at all.'

Mary's friend, Fleur Arnold, had the same problem, but she *behaved* in a different way. She thought about the *alternatives* for a long time, getting more and more information about each job. Finally, she *made up* her mind. She didn't phone the company, though. She waited for a few more days … and *changed* her mind. She still didn't accept the job, and finally she changed her *mind* again and *chose* the first job. However, she was not happy with her *decision*. 'I think the other job was better,' she says now.

Exercise D

Set for group work. Monitor.

Closure

Feed back on Exercise D, eliciting best examples.

Lesson 2: Speaking

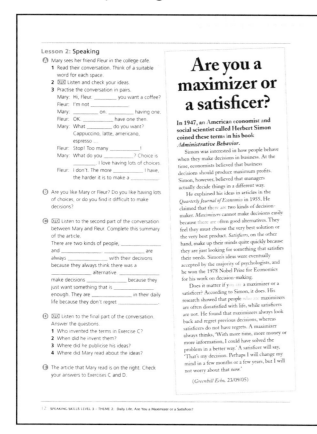

Introduction

Drill the green words from Lesson 1.

Remind students of the two characters from Lesson 1. Elicit their names. Note that the names exemplify one of the key skills of this theme – linking two vowels.

Mary /j/ *Orwell*
Fleur /r/ *Arnold*

Say the names with the linking but do not highlight at this point.

Exercise A

1   Set for individual work, then pairwork checking. Do not feed back.
2   Play the recording. Feed back, perhaps by building up the conversation on the board. Drill for pronunciation and intonation. Highlight the following, but don't say at this point what is happening:
   a   linkage from consonant to vowel in, e.g., *want a; choice is; lots of; choices I; it is; make a*
   b   linkage from vowel to vowel: *go /w/ on; latte /j/ Americano /w/ espresso; harder /r/ it*
3   Set for pairwork. Feed back, getting one or two groups to perform in front of the rest of the class.

Answers

Target words in italics

Mary: Hi, Fleur. *Do* you want a coffee?

Fleur: I'm not *sure*.

Mary: *Go* on. *I'm* having one.

Fleur: OK. *I'll* have one then.

Mary: What *kind* do you want? Cappuccino, latte, americano, espresso …

Fleur: Stop! Too many *choices*!

Mary: What do you *mean*? Choice is *good*. I love having lots of choices.

Fleur: I don't. The more *choices* I have, the harder it is to make a *decision*.

Exercise B

This is a continuation from the question in Lesson 1 Exercise D. However, the extra point here is – *do you like to have choice*? e.g., 10 different kinds of coffee. Set for pairwork. Feed back orally.

Exercise C

Give students time to look at the text. It is almost unintelligible, but at least prepares them a little for the listening. Set for pairwork. Play Part 2 of the recording. Do not feed back at this point. Students will be able to check their own work in Exercise E.

Exercise D

Give students time to look at the questions. Mention that these are key questions when you are doing research. Set for pairwork. Play Part 3 of the recording. Feed back orally. Mary, of course, cannot give any of this information. This points the way to Exercise E below and the third Skills Check in Lesson 3. Point out that you agree with Fleur – Mary should make a note of this information.

Exercise E

Set for individual work then pairwork checking. Tell students to ignore the coloured letters and words for the moment. Feed back on Exercise C, ideally onto an OHT of the text. Feed back orally on the questions in Exercise D.

Answers

C

Target words in italics

There are two kinds of people, *maximizers* and *satisficers*. *Maximizers* are always *unhappy* with their decisions because they always think there was a *better* alternative. *Satisficers* make decisions *easily* because they just want something that is *good* enough. They are *happier* in their daily life because they don't regret *decisions*.

D

1   Herbert Simon – an American economist and social scientist.
2   In 1947.
3   In a book called *Administrative Behavior* (US spelling) and in articles in the *Quarterly Journal of Economics*.
4   In the *Greenhill Echo* of 23rd September, 2005.

Closure

Do further high-speed comprehension work on the text. You can play 'Stupid Teacher', i.e., read the text, students' books open, and make stupid mistakes for students to correct. Pause after each stupid mistake for students to process what you said and correct. For example:

> Are you a maximizer or a satisficer?
> In 1497 ... an **Australian ecologist** ... called **Simon Herbert** ... coined these terms in his **article** ... *Administrative Behavior*. Simon was interested in how **animals** behave when they make decisions **in their social life** ... At the time, economists believed that business decisions should produce maximum **employment** ... Simon, however, believed that managers actually decide things in a different **place** ...

Methodology note

'Stupid Teacher', conducted in this way, is a good technique for improving integrated language processing. In order to correct your spoken mistakes, students must recognise the error – a listening skill – find the correct form in written language – a reading skill – and turn it into spoken correction. Alternatively, they can correct from memory, which is just listening and speaking.

Lesson 3: Learning new skills

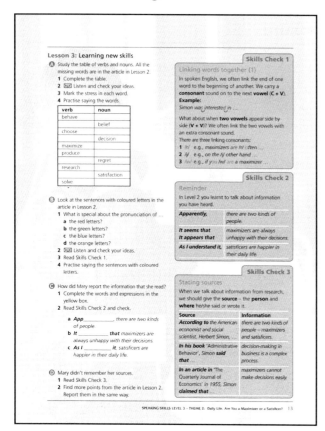

Exercise A

Refer students to the table.

1 Set for individual work then pairwork checking. Emphasise that the missing words are all in the article; therefore, if the students are stuck, they can look back and find a word with a related form and meaning in the article.

2 Play the recording. Feed back, building up the table on the board.

3 Set for individual work then pairwork checking. Play the recording again if you wish.

4 Drill chorally, then individually.

Answers

Target words in italics.

verb	noun
behave	*behaviour*
believe	belief
choose	*choice*
decide	decision
maximize	*maximum*
produce	*product*
regret	regret
research	*research*
satisfy	satisfaction
solve	*solution*

Introduction

Refer students to the green words. Allow them to read for one minute, then, if you wish, ask them to close their books. Ask them to identify words from specific sounds, i.e., which green words have the following sounds:

/ɪ/   *behave, decide* (the first *e*); *decision* (twice); *alternative; regret* (the first *e*)

/e/   *regret*

/uː/   *choose*

/eɪ/   *make; change; behave*

/aɪ/   *decide; mind*

/ɔː/   *alternative*

/ɜː/   *alternative*

/ə/   *decision; behave; alternative*

/z/   *choose*

/s/   *decide; decision*

/dʒ/   *change*

/tʃ/   *choose; change*

/ʒ/   *decision*

Methodology note

Recognising similarities of form is a key skill in language learning, e.g., *choose* and *choice* are related. It is also important to recognise the correct part of speech.

Exercise B

Refer students to the first paragraph of the article in Lesson 2 (with the red letters).

1 and 2 Set question 1a for whole-class work. Elicit ideas, then play the first section of the recording. Repeat the procedure for the other subsections of 1. Point out that the letter that makes the sound often occurs in the original word but is not pronounced normally, e.g., *are a* = the *r* is there but is not normally rolled.

3 Refer students to Skills Check 1. Be prepared to play all the sections again for students to really hear the linkage.

4 Drill chorally and individually some of the sentences with coloured letters.

Ask students to find more examples of each type of linking.

Answers

Target linking in italics

1a = C + V

In 1947, a*n* America*n* e*conomist* a*nd* social scientist called Herbert Simon coined these term*s* i*n* his boo*k* Administrative Behavior.

1b = V + /r/ + V

He claimed that th*ere are* two kinds of decision-maker. Maximizers cannot make decisions easily because *there are* often good alternatives.

1c = V + /j/ + V

Satisficers, on *the other* hand, make up their minds quite quickly because *they are* just looking for something that satisfies their needs.

1d = V + /w/ + V

Does it matter if *you are* a maximizer or a satisficer? According to Simon, it does. His research showed that people *who are* maximizers are often dissatisfied with life, while satisficers are not.

Additional examples:

1a = C + V

Lots of examples!

1b = V + /r/ + V

maximize*r or a* satisficer? we*re* eventually; fo*r* Economics; a*re* often; maximize*r a*lways; mo*re* information; o*r a* few

1c = V + /j/ + V

eventuall*y a*ccepted; majorit*y o*f; mone*y o*r

1d = V + /w/ + V

Are y*ou a* maximizer …?

Methodology note

Running the consonant at the end of one word into the vowel at the beginning of the next word produces a very 'English' sound. A phrase like *not at all* said with native-speaker pronunciation sounds more like *no ta tall* to many language learners. Recognising the existence of this linking is a key skill, therefore, for two reasons. Firstly, it improves pronunciation, and secondly, it enables better recognition in the stream of speech.

Language and culture note

Arabic has a glottal stop, so Arabs are quite prepared to use this between two vowels, e.g., the /glottal/ other. They are quite surprised to learn that a completely new consonant or semi-vowel sound appears in this environment.

Exercise C

Students who did Level 2 will be familiar with these ways of reporting without stating sources. It does not matter if your students didn't do Level 2, however, since there is a Skills Check Reminder.

1   Set for individual work then pairwork checking.
2   Refer students to Skills Check 2 for self-checking.

    Drill the phrases. Get students to report other information from the article using these phrases.

Answers

a   *Apparently, there are two kinds of people.*
b   *It seems that maximizers are always unhappy with their decisions.*
c   *As I understand it, satisficers are happier in their daily life.*

Exercise D

Remind students that Mary didn't remember her sources.

1   Refer students to Skills Check 3. Work through the points there. Point out the difference between just saying the person (the first phrase) and giving the printed source (phrases two and three). When we are reporting research, we should always give the printed source, so other people can go and read more deeply, or simply check that we have reported accurately. Drill the phrases.
2   Set for pairwork. Feed back orally.

Closure

Make the following statements in random order and ask students which kind of person would say each one – a maximizer or a satificer.

Maximizer	Satisficer
I just can't decide.	*I don't mind. I'll have tea or coffee.*
It's so hard to choose.	*You can't go back, can you?*
Could you help me with this decision?	*I've never done anything I regret.*
I wonder if I did the right thing?	*When I go shopping for something, I'm in and out of the shop in a few minutes.*

Ask students if they think they are maximizers or satisficers.

Lesson 4: Applying skills

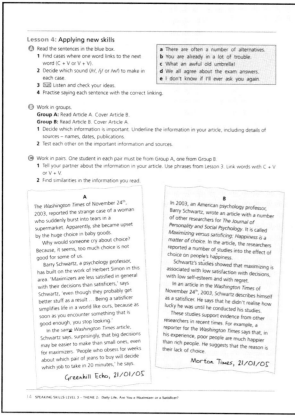

c   What an awful old umbrella!
d   We all agree about the exam answers.
e   I don't know if I'll ever ask you again.

Exercise B

Set for group work. You may need to give each group a lot of help to understand the text. Encourage the students to ask each other and you about the meaning and pronunciation of new words using good English – form and pronunciation.

Exercise C

1   Set for pairwork. Monitor and assist. Make notes of linking problems and failure to use correct sourcing phrases. Feed back on this with individual students at the end.
2   This could be done as a whole-class activity.

Introduction

Remind students about linking from Lesson 3. Use the two names to introduce the topic (*Mary Orwell* and *Fleur Arnold*) and the question from the beginning of the article in Lesson 2 that contains a lot of linking – *Are you a maximizer or a satisficer?*

Closure

Test students on the information they heard about rather than read about. Ask students from Group A questions about Article B and vice versa.

Exercise A

1 and 2 Set for individual work then pairwork checking.
3   Play the sentences. Drill chorally and individually after each one.
4   Set for pairwork. Monitor and assist.

Answers

Linking of underlined items.
a   There are often a number of alternatives.
b   You are already in a lot of trouble.

Lesson 1: Vocabulary

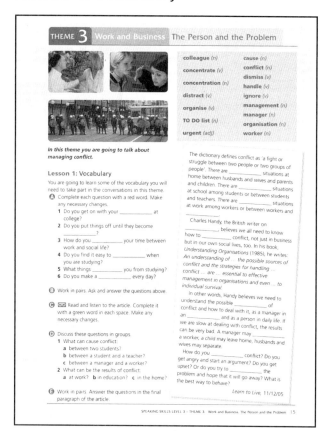

What is the sound of *g* in the first word? /g/
What is the sound of the first and then the second *c* in the next two words? /k/; /s/
How do you often say this combination – *a_e*? /eɪ/
How do you often say this combination – *i_e*? /aɪ/
How do you usually say *g* in front of *e*? /dʒ/

Invite students to try to say the words. Confirm and correct. Drill.

Exercise A

Set for individual work then pairwork checking. Feed back orally. Elicit a meaning for each of the words and phrases.

Answers

1   Do you get on with your *colleagues* at college?
2   Do you put things off until they become *urgent*?
3   How do you *organise* your time between work and social life?
4   Do you find it easy to *concentrate* when you are studying?
5   What things *distract* you from studying?
6   Do you make a *to do list* every day?

Exercise B

Set for pairwork. Feed back orally.

Exercise C

Refer students to the diagram on the board again. Explain that they are now going to hear something to help them understand this diagram.

Set for individual work. Refer students to the green words. Give them some time to read them, but do not deal with pronunciation or meaning at this point.

Introduction

Draw the following diagram on the board.

Conflict

Person   Problem

Tell students that this is the theme of this unit, but do not explain anything. Say you will come back to this later and ask the students to try to explain the diagram. Do not erase it.

Refer students to the red words. As always, point out that these are words from this theme at Level 2. Ask students to mark the stress on the words and phrases – note that even the phrase has a main stress (on *DO*). Deal with a few potential pronunciation traps as follows:

Play the recording, with students following in their books. Pause occasionally to give students time to complete the writing. Feed back, asking individual students to read out sentences with the correct 'missing' word. Work on the linking of sounds that the students covered in the previous theme, particularly the first one below:

C + V, e.g., *The dictionary defines <u>conflict as 'a</u> <u>fight or</u> struggle …*

V + /r/ + V e.g., <u>*There are*</u> *conflict situations; in <u>our</u> <u>own</u> social lives.*

V + /j/ + V e.g., *If <u>we are</u> slow at dealing with conflict …*

V + /w/ + V e.g., *Handy believes we need <u>to</u> <u>understand</u> …*

Do not do much work on meaning at this stage. Lack of comprehension will emerge in later activities.

Answer

Target words in italics.
The dictionary defines conflict as 'a fight or struggle between two people or two groups of people'. There are *conflict* situations at home between husbands and wives and parents and children. There are *conflict* situations at school among students or between students and teachers. There are *conflict* situations at work, among workers or between workers and *managers*.

Charles Handy, the British writer on *management*, believes we all need to know how to *handle* conflict, not just in business but in our own social lives, too. In his book, *Understanding Organisations* (1985), he writes:

An understanding of … the possible sources of conflict and the strategies for handling … conflict, … are … essential to effective management in organisations and even … to individual survival.
In other words, Handy believes we need to understand the possible *causes* of conflict and how to deal with it,

as a manager in an *organisation*, and as a person in daily life. If we are slow at dealing with conflict, the results can be very bad. A manager may *dismiss* a worker, a child may leave home, husbands and wives may separate.

How do **you** *handle* conflict? Do you get angry and start an argument? Do you get upset? Or do you try to *ignore* the problem and hope that it will go away? What is the best way to behave? *Learn to Live* 11/12/05

Methodology notes

1   Listening and reading at the same time is a very good way to train the ear, which in turn will monitor the mouth in speaking.
2   Reading aloud is not an easy speaking skill, but it is a key one, particularly for students. In a study environment, it is often necessary for students to read from research works or from their own writing. We should not demand any performance ability in the reading aloud, but we can look for accurate sound–sight identification.

Language and culture note

People from cultures with a tradition of rote learning are very good at retaining an aural memory of words and phrases. If you can give such people an aural trace of a word as they read it, they are more likely to be able to pronounce it correctly, by simple mimicry, later.

Role play

Set up a role play as follows:

Student A: You have read the article on the right. Tell Student B about it. State your sources.

Student B: Listen and check information.

Remind students about the ways of stating sources from Theme 2. Note that in this role play Student B could be completely passive and the whole thing would not be communicative, as there would be no information gap. Show, therefore, how Student B can be more active – by misunderstanding what Student A says and questioning sources, if Student A does not give them. Write some possible sentences for Student B on the board:

> Misunderstanding:
> *I thought you said ...*
> *I see. So Handy says ...*
> *Did you say ...?*
> *Sorry. Could you go over that bit again?*
> Questioning sources:
> *Where did you read this?*
> *Who said that?*
> *What was the name of the book?*
> *When was it published?*

Monitor the role play, assisting as necessary, then feed back, highlighting interesting exchanges.

Exercise D

Set for pairwork. Monitor and assist. Feed back orally.

Answers
Possible answers

1 causes of conflict
   a between two students = problems in halls of residence
   b between student and teacher = student coming late; not handing in assignment
   c between manager and worker = worker coming late; not doing work properly

2 results of conflict
   a people are dismissed or leave a job
   b students get bad marks or leave a school / college
   c parents don't talk to each other, divorce, children leave home

Exercise E

Set for pairwork. Monitor. Make notes of interesting answers.

Closure

Feed back orally, eliciting the best answers.

Lesson 2: Speaking

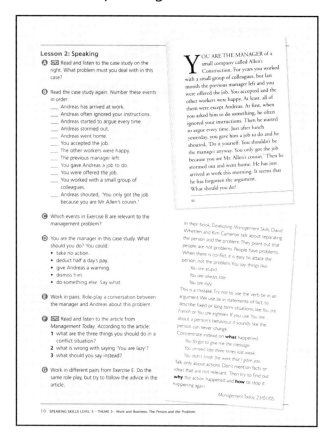

Exercise A

Redraw the diagram from Lesson 1 and remind students that this is what the theme is about. Elicit the meaning of *conflict* and point out that by the end of the lesson they will be able to explain the diagram.

Explain that management writers often talk about *case studies* – write the expression on the board. Explain that a case study is a particular situation with a management problem. You read the situation and you work out the best solution to the problem.

Set for pairwork. Play the recording. Students listen and read at the same time. Elicit ideas on the problem. Do not confirm or correct.

Exercise B

Set for pairwork. Use cut-ups of the sentences if possible. Feed back, ideally with an OHT of the sentences in the correct order. During the feedback, check that students are linking correctly, e.g., as follows:

C + V
Andreas has arrived at work.
Andreas often ignored your instructions.
Andreas stormed out.
You gave Andreas a job to do.

V + /r/ + V
Andreas often ignored your instructions.
You were offered the job.

V + /j/ + V
The other workers were happy.

V + /w/ + V
Andreas started to argue every time.
You accepted the job.
Andreas shouted, 'You only got the job because you are Mr. Allen's cousin.'

Introduction

Get students to mark the stress on the multi-syllable green words in Lesson 1. Elicit pronunciation from individual students. Check the following points:

cause	pronunciation of *au* = not /aʊ/, but /ɔː/
conflict	stress and clusters – *fl*; *ct*
handle	lateral plosion of the *dle* cluster – the tongue stays in the place of articulation for *d* and air is exploded sideways
ignore	pronunciation of *g*
management	pronunciation of *g*
manager	pronunciation of *g*; no rolling of *r*
organisation	pronunciation of *s*
worker	no pronunciation of first *r* or rolling of second *r*

Drill chorally and individually.

Answers

Correct order:

You worked with a small group of colleagues.
The previous manager left.
You were offered the job.
You accepted the job.
The other workers were happy.
Andreas often ignored your instructions.
Andreas started to argue every time.
You gave Andreas a job to do.
Andreas shouted, 'You only got the job because you are Mr. Allen's cousin.'
Andreas stormed out.
Andreas went home.
Andreas has arrived at work.

Exercise C

Explain the word *relevant* = something that is important in a particular situation. Point out that you must always concentrate on the things that are important in a case study, and ignore the things that are not important. Explain that it is sometimes difficult to work out in a conflict what is important, in business and in our daily lives.

Set for pairwork. Feed back orally. Do not confirm or correct at this point. Ideally, get the students arguing with each about what is important, using available linguistic resources. This is a good precursor to Lesson 3 Skills Check 2.

Exercise D

Explain that you can't solve a problem until you have decided what the problem is. So now students should be in a good position to decide what to do in this situation.

Check that they understand all the choices – and the fact that they can make other choices too. Note: *deduct* is a new word and will need careful teaching. Elicit

ideas from individuals, or put into groups first if you wish. Once again, an argument between students / groups would be good.

Exercise E

Set up the pairwork carefully. Point out that the manager needs to decide the problem and the solution before the conversation. Point out that, in this situation, Andreas would be expecting something to happen, so he can also prepare what he is going to say in the conversation. Give the students some time to prepare the role play.

Monitor. Get some of the most interesting pairs to perform in front of the class.

Exercise F

Ask students if they think they identified the problem well and dealt with the situation in the best way. Point out that they are now going to read some theory about this.

Set for pairwork. Give students time to read the questions. Play the recording. Students listen and follow in their books. Feed back. Point out that concentrating on what happened is about looking at relevant facts and ignoring the things that are not important. Ask again about the facts in the case study. See if students have changed their minds about what is relevant.

Answers

1 Concentrate on *what* happened, *why* it happened and *how* to stop it happening again.
2 You are concentrating on the person, not the problem. You are suggesting the person cannot change.
3 *You did not finish the work I gave you.* or *You did not work hard enough last week.*

The only relevant fact here is that Andreas did not follow your instructions. You are the manager. Of course, you must not ask your workers to do stupid things or overwork them, but if your instructions are sensible, then workers must obey them. If they cannot do that, they must leave. The best course of action here is to give him a warning and explain that if he does it again, he will have to leave.

Exercise G

Follow the procedure from Exercise E. Monitor.

Closure

Get pairs with the best role plays to perform them for the class.

Ask students to explain the diagram on the board now.

Lesson 3: Learning new skills

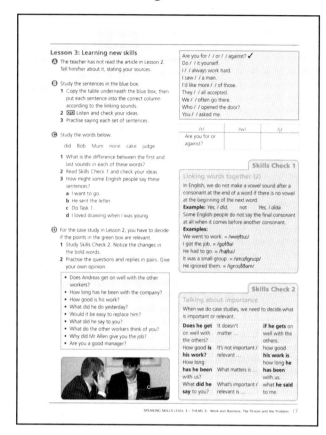

Introduction

See how much students can remember about the case study in Lesson 2. Try to elicit the full information, then the relevant facts. Check linking as students speak, but do not interrupt the flow. Feed back later on individual points.

Exercise A

Pretend that you have not read the article. Ask students to tell you about it, and make sure they state the sources. If necessary, refer them back to the structures in Theme 2 Lesson 3.

Exercise B

Copy the table onto the board and write the example in. Highlight the /r/ sound in the two places indicated by the / /.

/r/	/w/	/j/
Are you for or against?		

1   Elicit the correct answer for the second sentence. Ask students to copy the table into their notebooks and complete the activity.
2   Play the recording, pausing after each sentence for students to check / correct.
3   Drill the sentences, chorally and individually.

Answers

/r/	/w/	/j/
I saw a man.	You asked me.	They all accepted.
Are you for or against?	Do it yourself.	We often go there.
I'd like more of those.	Who opened the door?	I always work hard.

Exercise C

1   Write the word *did* on the board and set the question. Elicit answers, if any, but do not confirm or correct. Refer students to the words in the box. Make sure that the students understand the question is about sounds not spelling, e.g., *none* has /n/ at the beginning and the end.
2   Set for individual work then pairwork checking.
3   Set for pairwork. Feed back onto the board. Point out that this feature of pronunciation means that you sometimes don't hear the regular past tense ending of verbs because the /t/ or /d/ are not exploded. Examples:

He ignored them.
She asked John.
I liked drawing.

Answers

1   The second last sound is not exploded –
    demonstrate.

3   They might pronounce the key sections as:
    a   /wɒntə/
    b   /senðə/
    c   /tɑːswʌn/
    d   /lʌvdrɔː/

Methodology note

It is not necessary to drill the full suppressed
plosives, such as those shown in the second half of
the Skills Check, since this is a Speaking course.
Non-native speakers certainly do not have to
produce all the features of native speech to be
understood, which is the aim of the exercise.
However, for interactive spoken work, it is
obviously important that a student should be able
to recognise *small* in the phrase *Get into small
groups* even though the native speaker does not
pronounce the dark *l* of *small*. Later in the course
we look at cases where completely new sounds
appear, e.g., *hand* in a phrase like *Could you hand
back your books?* may become *ham*, i.e., *Could
you hamback your books?*

Exercise D

Remind students of the case study in Lesson 2. Remind
them also that they had to work out which facts were
relevant.

1   Set for individual reading. Work carefully through
    the word changes and word order changes with
    diagrams on the board.

2   Drill the activity with open pairs. Set for pairwork.
    Monitor and assist.

Answers

Pattern exchange:

S1: Does Andreas get on well with the other workers?

S2: It doesn't matter if he gets on well with the other
    workers. What's important is what he said to me.

Closure

Ask the questions in the first column. Elicit responses
from individual students.

Lesson 4: Applying new skills

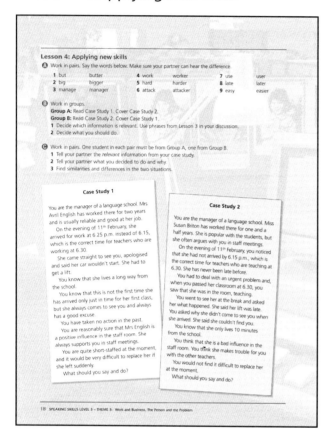

Language and culture note

Stops are not generally exploded in final position in Arabic, so this should not be a great problem for Arabic speakers. However, some Arabic speakers use something similar to schwa as a hesitation device at the end of a content word, e.g., *I wenta to the banka and gota some money.*

Exploding like this can cause confusion in a listener's mind, as this exercise shows. In English, we tend to use the same hesitation device after the article or other function words, e.g., *Ia went to thea bank anda got somea money.*

Exercise B

Follow the same procedure as in Theme 2. Make absolutely sure that students understand the main points of the case study in their groups and then decide what is relevant. Encourage them to use the phrases from Lesson 3. Monitor and see if students are exploding stops when they should not be. Do not confirm and correct ideas on what is relevant at this stage.

Introduction

Ask some questions about the case study from Lesson 2, using the questions from Skills Check 2 (Lesson 3).

Exercise A

Remind students about the pronunciation of a consonant at the end of a word.

Point out that there is a difference between *but* and *butter.*

Drill the pairs of words, chorally and individually.

Set for pairwork. One student says one word from each pair. The other student identifies which word is being said. Monitor and check that students really can say the two words in a markedly different way.

Exercise C

Follow the same procedure as in Theme 2. Monitor and assist.

Get feed back on the similarities and differences in the *relevant* facts. The chances are that students will raise other facts as being relevant but, in strictly management terms, they are not. You should not make a decision on what to say or do about, e.g., a person's lateness based on:

- their attitude to you;
- where a person lives relative to the business;
- rumours about a person (e.g., you are reasonably sure that …);
- how easy it is to replace a person.

Of course, you may wish to discuss attitude at the same meeting, although, ideally, it should be the subject of a meeting as soon as you notice it, not brought up as 'and another thing' in a meeting to discuss lateness.

Answers

The only really relevant fact in Case Study 1 is that Mrs English has come in late several times. You must find out why this has happened and how you can stop it happening in the future.

The only really relevant fact in Case Study 2 is that Miss Briton has never been late before. You must find out why this has happened and how you can stop it happening in the future.

Closure

Get students to role-play the meeting with their employee – Mrs English or Miss Briton. Monitor. Get the best pairs to perform in front of the class.

Lesson 1: Vocabulary

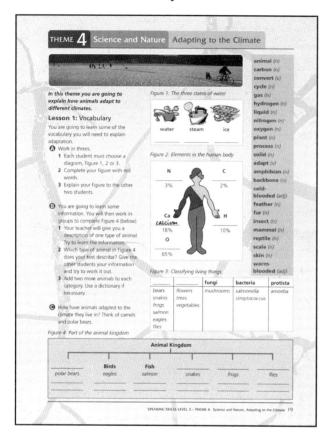

Introduction

If students did Theme 4 of Level 2 (about the natural cycles on Earth) elicit as much information as possible about the nitrogen cycle and the carbon and oxygen cycle. If they did not do this theme, do not try to explain anything about these cycles now.

If students did not do that theme / level, go straight into Exercise A, which adequately revises the key words.

Refer students to the red words. Do not deal with meaning at this time, but ask students to mark the stress on multi-syllable words. Feed back individually, then drill the words chorally and individually. Point out that the stress in *con'vert* is on the second syllable because it is a verb. There is a two-syllable noun *'convert*, which means a person who has changed religion or ideas about something. Point out that the stress in *'process* is on the first syllable because it is a noun. You do not need to mention that there are

two-syllable verbs, *'process*, which means to put through a system, and *pro'cess*, which means to walk ceremonially.

Exercise A

1   Put students into threes. Make sure one student in each group is doing each figure.
2   Monitor and assist.
3   Monitor. Students who are listening close their books. Encourage students to be accurate in their descriptions and check that listening students have understood. Remind students that they can ask about the meaning of things, and get students to repeat things they don't understand – this previews one of the target sub-skills of this theme.

Feed back with model descriptions of each figure. Perhaps elicit ideas from students and draw or construct on the board, making mistakes if students are inaccurate in their descriptions. Deal with extra stuff, such as *bacteria* = things which can hurt you or help you, but don't worry about low-cover points like *protista*. However, students should be able to make a stab at pronouncing the words, using available knowledge of sound–sight relationships in English.

Answers
Figure 1: The three states of water

water   steam   ice

liquid   gas   solid

Figure 2: Elements in the human body

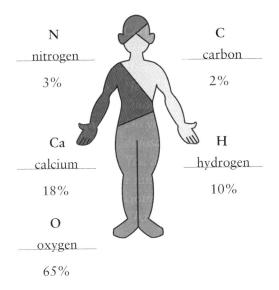

N	C
nitrogen	carbon
3%	2%
Ca	H
calcium	hydrogen
18%	10%
O	
oxygen	
65%	

Figure 3: Classifying living things

animals	plants	fungi	bacteria	protista
bears snakes frogs salmon eagles flies	flowers trees vegetables	mushrooms	salmonella strepto- coccus	amoeba

Language and culture note

The names of some elements – especially those derived from Greek – are virtually the same in Arabic, e.g., *oxygen, hydrogen, nitrogen, carbon.* In addition, many students will be familiar with the use of the first letter or letters (*O, H*, etc.) in chemical equations

The word *salmon* (pronounced with the *l*) also exists in Arabic and is, in fact, the root of the name *Suleiman*.

Exercise B

Refer students to Figure 4 for the names of the animals.

The descriptions of the animals are printed on page 55 of this Teacher's Book. Copy the descriptions and hand them out on individual pieces of paper.

1   Put students into groups to study one animal each – i.e., you are going to have six groups altogether at this stage. Monitor and assist, but as far as possible get students to help each other to understand the text. Explain that they will not be able to look at the text in the next stage, so they must try to learn the information.

2   Put students into groups with at least one person from each of the six groups in Exercise B1. Refer them to Figure 4. Point out that *Fish* is a singular and a plural word. Explain the use of the word *kingdom*. Point out that there is also a *plant kingdom*, a *fungi kingdom*, etc. It is the next level of classification. Ask them to complete the table with green words. Feed back, building up the table on the board. Check the stress of the green words.

3   Do as a whole class, adding animals as they are suggested, even if they are wrong, then elicit comments from other students. End with a model version.

Answers
1 and 2
    A   Insects
    B   Amphibians
    C   Reptiles
    D   Fish
    E   Birds
    F   Mammals

3 *Figure 4: Part of the animal kingdom*

Animal Kingdom

Mammals   Birds   Fish   Reptiles   Amphibians   Insects
polar bears   eagles   salmon   snakes   frogs   flies

Methodology note

Strictly speaking, the names here are not the class names for subdividing the Animal Kingdom. However, the scientific words are too low-cover for a general course of this nature.

Note also that, e.g., spiders and scorpions are not insects but *arachnids*, as they have eight legs and two body parts, but once again this is added complexity. Mention that this is a simplified system, if the point comes up.

Exercise C

Refer students to the title of this theme – *Adapting to the Climate*. Elicit the meaning of *climate* (the pattern of weather in a particular area) and explain that in this theme you are going to look at the way animals have adapted – or changed – to be able to live in different climates. Ask students to tell you the two most difficult climates to live in (elicit *the poles* and *the deserts*). Make sure students know what a camel is – if you have any problems there is a picture in Lesson 4.

Set for pairwork. Feed back orally. Do not confirm or correct at this stage. If students say things like *Camels can store water in their humps* (false), let it stand. Simply say that you will check the facts later in the theme.

Closure

Drill the green words for pronunciation, especially stress.

PHOTOCOPIABLE

A
They do not have a backbone. They are cold-blooded. They have six legs and three body parts. Some of them can fly. They change shape during their life cycle.

B
They have a backbone. They are cold-blooded. They have smooth wet skin. They spend part of their life in water and part of it on land. They lay eggs.

C
They have a backbone. They are cold-blooded. They have dry skin and scales. They breathe air. Some of them do not have any arms or legs.

D
They have a backbone. They are warm-blooded. They have scales. They breathe in water. They lay eggs that contain food for the young animals.

E
They have a backbone. They are warm-blooded. They breathe air. They have feathers. Most of them can fly. They lay eggs that contain food for the young animals.

F
They have a backbone. They are warm-blooded. They usually have hair or fur. They breathe air. They give birth to live young and make milk to feed their young.

Lesson 2: Speaking

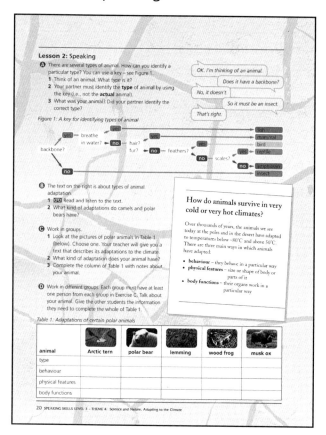

Introduction

Remind students of the green words from Lesson 1. Check pronunciation, perhaps with a quiz, e.g.,

which words have at least one schwa?
adapt; amphibian; feather; mammal

have an /ɪ/ sound?
amphibian; cold-blooded; insect; skin; warm-blooded

have an /æ/ sound?
adapt; amphibian; backbone; mammal

have a /f/ sound?
amphibian; feather; fur

You can allow the students to look at the words, since it is sound–sight that you are trying to reinforce with this exercise.

Work also on the clusters and suppressed plosives in all these words:

adapt; amphibian; backbone; cold-blooded; warm-blooded; insect; reptile; scale; skin

Exercise A

Remind students of the different types of animals from Lesson 1. Elicit example animals of each type.

Work through the conversation on the right of the page, showing how it takes information from the key (Figure 1). Highlight the use of *must* for deduction. You can also teach *can't* as the opposite.

Think of an animal yourself and work through the activity as an example.

Set for pairwork. Monitor. Feed back with some good examples from pairs.

Exercise B

1   Set for individual work then pairwork checking. Play the recording. Feed back, checking comprehension of the text.
2   Refer students back to the polar bear and the camel question from Lesson 1. They should be able to classify their examples in terms of behaviour, physical features or body functions. Do not spend long on this, unless students have a lot to say.

Exercise C

Follow the procedure from Lesson 1 for this kind of activity.
1   Make sure that there are at least six groups, with each animal being studied by at least one group. The texts are printed at the back of the Course Book (pages 59–63) as well as on page 58 of this Teacher's Book. As before, ideally give out the texts

on separate pieces of paper. Encourage students to help each other with the text.

2   Monitor and assist.

3   Monitor and assist.

Exercise D

Follow the procedure from Lesson 1 for this kind of activity.

Make sure that at least one student in each group has studied each animal. They should not look back at the text unless they get really stuck.

Feed back, ideally onto an OHT of the table; otherwise, build up a model version on the board.

Answers
Model table

animal	Arctic tern	polar bear	lemming	wood frog	musk ox
type	bird	mammal	mammal	amphibian	mammal
behaviour	migrates	sleeps for large parts of the winter – hibernates	burrows under the snow and ice	deep hibernation	huddles with other animals
physical features		thick fur in the winter; thick layer of fat = insulates	has a small body and thick skin to keep in the heat	cold-blooded = does not need to keep temperature high	thick hair in the winter
body functions		breathing and heart rate slows down		breathing and heartbeat stops; special chemical in blood stops it from freezing	

Closure

Ask students questions about each of the animals in Exercise D. All the questions should come from the identification key in Exercise 1 of this lesson or from the information about each type of animal in Lesson 1. After a few seconds they should realise that they can answer the questions because they know which type of animal is involved.

Example questions: *Does the musk ox give birth to live young? Does it produce milk? Is it cold-blooded? Does it have a backbone?*

The Arctic tern is a bird. It has not really adapted to the cold at all. It lives at the North Pole in the summer months, but as the weather starts to get colder, it migrates to the South Pole. Migrate means *move to live in another place*. The weather at the South Pole, of course, is starting to get warmer at this time because the seasons are reversed in the southern hemisphere.

The polar bear is a mammal. It has adapted to the cold in several ways. Firstly, the animal has a thick layer of fat under the skin. Fat is a good insulator, which means it stops the body heat of the animal escaping. Secondly, in the winter the polar bear grows thicker fur. Finally, the polar bear sleeps for large parts of the winter. It hibernates, which means its breathing and heart rate slow down.

The lemming is a tiny mammal. It has adapted to the cold in several ways. Firstly, it burrows or digs deep under the snow or ice. The temperature a few metres underground is much warmer because snow and ice are good insulators. In other words, they keep out the cold. Secondly, the lemming has a small body and a thick skin. When it rolls up inside its tiny burrow, it keeps most of its body heat inside.

The wood frog is an amphibian. It is cold-blooded, which means that it does not have to keep up a high body temperature, but it has adapted to the cold in another amazing way. As the temperature falls, the wood frog goes into deep hibernation. Hibernation is a state in which the animal stops breathing and the heart stops beating. The blood temperature of the wood frog falls to around -5°C, but a special chemical in the blood stops it from freezing and damaging the blood vessels.

The musk ox is a mammal. It has adapted to the cold in two main ways. Firstly, it grows thick hair in winter. Secondly, musk oxen (the plural of ox) are herd animals, like cows and goats, which means that they live together in large groups. In the winter they huddle together so that the herd becomes one large body with only a small surface area to lose heat.

Lesson 3: Learning new skills

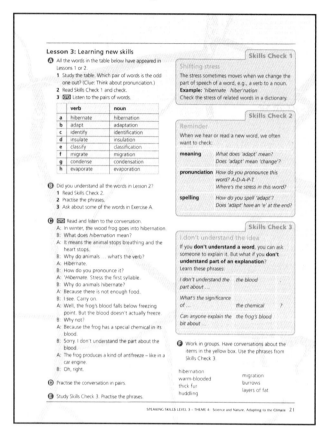

The odd one out is *migrate/migration* because the stress does not move.

verb	noun
1 'hibernate	hiber'nation
2 a'dapt	adap'tation
3 i'dentify	identifi'cation
4 'insulate	insu'lation
5 'classify	classifi'cation
6 mi'grate	mi'gration
7 con'dense	conden'sation
8 e'vaporate	evapo'ration

Language and culture note

There is an 80% rule in English that in multi-syllable words the stress is on the ante-penultimate syllable (i.e., third from the end), e.g., *sig'nificance*, *'physical*, *am'phibian*. Words ending in *-ation* probably followed this pattern at one time and were pronounced *'a ti on*. Over the centuries the last two syllables have become one so that the stress is now on the penultimate syllable.

Introduction

Build up on the board the animal identification key again (Figure 1 from Lesson 2 Exercise 1). Play the game again.

Exercise A

1 and 2 Set for individual work then pairwork checking.
3   Play the recording.

Feed back building up the table on the board and marking the stress. Drill chorally and individually. Point out that a lot of English nouns end in *ation*. Nouns are often built from verbs in this way if the verbs ends in *-ate*, e.g., *lubricate, excavate, renovate*. Nouns are often built with *-ication* from verbs ending *-fy*, e.g., *specify, justify, exemplify* (but note *satisfy / satisfaction*).

Exercise B

Students at Level 1 learnt how to use these phrases, but the reminder might be timely.

Set for pairwork. Feed back orally.

Exercise C

Set for individual work. Play the recording. Drill the key phrases and exchanges. Note that there is a preview of the Skills Check 3 idea (not understanding one of the ideas).

Exercise D

Set for pairwork. Monitor and assist.

Exercise E

Set for pairwork. Drill the phrases, chorally and individually.

Exercise F

Set for pairwork. Monitor.

Closure

Feed back, getting some of the pairs to demonstrate good example conversations.

Lesson 4: Applying new skills

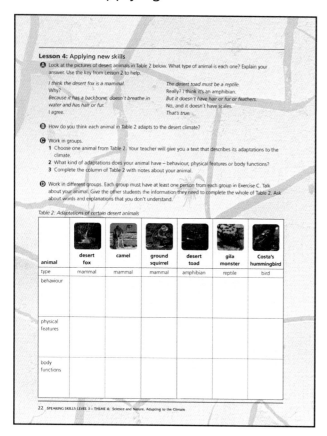

Lesson 4: Applying new skills

Ⓐ Look at the pictures of desert animals in Table 2 below. What type of animal is each one? Explain your answer. Use the key from Lesson 2 to help.

I think the desert fox is a mammal.
Why?
Because it has a backbone, doesn't breathe in water and has hair or fur.
I agree.

The desert toad must be a reptile.
Really? I think it's an amphibian.
But it doesn't have hair or fur or feathers.
No, and it doesn't have scales.
That's true.

Ⓑ How do you think each animal in Table 2 adapts to the desert climate?

Ⓒ Work in groups.
1 Choose one animal from Table 2. Your teacher will give you a text that describes its adaptations to the climate.
2 What kind of adaptations does your animal have – behaviour, physical features or body functions?
3 Complete the column of Table 2 with notes about your animal.

Ⓓ Work in different groups. Each group must have at least one person from each group in Exercise C. Talk about your animal. Give the other students the information they need to complete the whole of Table 2. Ask about words and explanations that you don't understand.

Table 2: Adaptations of certain desert animals

animal	desert fox	camel	ground squirrel	desert toad	gila monster	Costa's hummingbird
type	mammal	mammal	mammal	amphibian	reptile	bird
behaviour						
physical features						
body functions						

22 SPEAKING SKILLS LEVEL 3 – THEME 4: Science and Nature. Adapting to the Climate

Introduction

Present the idea that you don't understand the concepts from the box in Lesson 3 Exercise F – listed below:

- *migration*
- *hibernation*
- *warm-blooded*
- *thick fur*
- *huddling*
- *burrows*
- *layers of fat*

Use phrases from the Skills Check and elicit explanations, e.g.,

> *In the text about the Arctic tern I don't understand the part about migration.*

Exercise A

Remind students about the identification key in Lesson 2.

Work through the example conversations.

Set for pairwork. Feed back orally, but don't confirm or correct. Students will find out later what type of animal each one is.

Exercise B

Remind students about the three kinds of adaptation – behaviour, physical features and body functions. Set for pairwork. Feed back orally, but don't confirm or correct. Students will find out later what adaptations each creature has.

Exercises C and D

Follow the procedure from Lesson 2 for these two activities. The texts are printed at the end of the Course Book (pages 59–64) as well as on page 64 of this Teacher's Book.

Closure

Get students to read out the texts they studied. Check their ability to link sounds and suppress plosives.

Answers

Model table

Table 2: Adaptations of certain desert animals

animal	desert fox	camel	ground squirrel	desert toad	gila monster	Costa's humming-bird
type	mammal	mammal	mammal	amphibian	reptile	bird
behaviour	nocturnal		estivates in summer + hibernates in winter	burrows into the ground; remains dormant	runs very fast = hot sand does not burn its feet; always stops in shade	migrates in late spring when temperatures become extreme
physical features	long ears with lots of blood vessels = good evaporation = loss of heat	long legs = lifts animal + good evaporation almost no fat under its skin = good evaporation				
body functions	eyes can see in the dark	stores fat in hump	temperature drops; heart rate falls to a few beats per minute; breathing slows down	body can store fat and water for long periods	can store fat in its tail	gets liquid directly from food = insects = from desert plants

PHOTOCOPIABLE

Costa's hummingbird is, of course, a bird. In some ways, it does not adapt to the heat of the desert climate because it migrates in late spring when the temperatures become extreme. However, it does have one important adaptation to the lack of water in the desert. The hummingbird is able to get liquid directly from the insects that it eats. The insects in turn get liquid from desert plants, which are, surprisingly, often full of water.

The gila monster is a reptile. It has two main adaptations to the desert climate. Firstly, it runs very fast across the hot sand so it does not burn its feet. It always stops in the shade. Secondly, the animal can store fat in its tail to help it survive long periods with no food or water.

Desert toads are amphibians. They have three main adaptations to the desert climate. Firstly, they burrow deep into the ground. The temperatures are much lower a few metres below the surface. Secondly, they lie dormant or not moving during periods with no rainfall. When the rain eventually fills up the desert ponds, the toads emerge from their burrows. Finally, their bodies can store fat and water for long periods.

The ground squirrel is a mammal. It is very well adapted to the extreme climate of the desert in which it lives. In the winter, when temperatures are very low at night, it *hibernates*. This means its body temperature drops to 0°C, its heart rate falls to a few beats per minute and its breathing slows down dramatically. In addition, it hibernates in the summer when temperatures are very high. This summer hibernation is called *estivation*.

The camel is a mammal that is perfectly adapted to the desert climate. Firstly, it has long legs that lift it high above the desert surface. At ground level the temperature can reach 90°C, whereas at the height of the camel's head it can be 40°C lower. The long legs also help the animal to lose heat. The large surface area encourages evaporation. Secondly, the camel has almost no fat under its skin. Once again, therefore, it loses heat easily, because fat is an insulator. Finally, the animal stores fat in its hump – not water as some people say, although it can drink over 100 litres of water at one time.

The desert fox is a mammal that is well adapted to the desert climate. Firstly, it is *nocturnal*, which means it only comes out at night when the temperature is lower. Secondly, its eyes can see very well in the dark. Finally, it has very large ears that are full of blood vessels. This gives the animal a large surface area for evaporation and loss of heat.

Lesson 1: Vocabulary

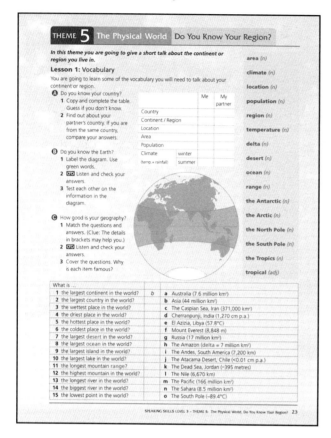

Introduction

Write the title of the theme on the board – *The Physical World*. Ask students to name words that they expect to occur in this lesson. Start the ball rolling with a few – *river, lake, island* … This activity will not only activate the required schemata, it will also give you a good idea of the range of the students' vocabulary in this area. Write the words on the board. Drill the main ones. Don't worry if some green words appear.

Refer students to the illustrations and check that they understand the new green words – *range, delta* and *ocean* – as well as the other items that they should know already.

Exercise A

If students did Level 2, remind them about the talk they gave about their own country, and how they

compared it with other countries in the region. If they didn't do Level 2, point out that it is very important to be able to give information about your own country and the continent or region it is in.

1 Set for individual work. Make sure students understand the kind of information they must put in each section. Write the points of the compass on the board. Make sure students can say, e.g., *My country is north of X; It is bordered on the east by Y / It has a border on the east with Y*. Write the units of measurement on the board and check, i.e., square kilometres (as km²), degrees centigrade (as °C), centimetres per year (as cm p.a.), millions (as m) or thousands (as k).

2 If students come from different countries, try to put them into pairs of different nationalities. They must cover their own table and ask questions to elicit information about their partner's country to complete the final column. If the students come from the same country, get them to compare the information, e.g., *What did you put for / have you got for …? Do you know (the area)?* Write some language on the board for guidance.

Feed back with comparatives:
– students from different countries, e.g., *X is bigger than Y; The population is smaller in X than in Y*, etc.
– students from the same country, e.g., *He thinks X is … but I think it's bigger*, etc.

Drill the pronunciation of the red words, especially the stress and schwas.

Exercise B

Copy the diagram of the globe on the board or use an OHT.
1 Set for individual work then pairwork checking.
2 Play the recording for students to check.

Feed back by eliciting answers and labelling the globe on the board or OHT.

Drill the green words, especially for stress and schwas. Demonstrate how intrusive sounds appear in *the /j/ Arctic*, *the /j/ Antarctic* and *the /j/ Equator*.

Exercise C

1 Set for pairwork. Demonstrate how the detailed figures can help to work out which question some of the answers belong to. Feed back orally. Do not confirm or correct.
2 Play the recording. Feed back, ideally onto an OHT of the correct answers.
3 Ask the questions to the whole class or set for pairwork. Monitor.

Answers

What is ...	Answer	Detail
1 the largest continent in the world?	Asia	44 million km²
2 the largest country in the world?	Russia	17 million km²
3 the wettest place in the world?	Cherranpunji, India	1,270 cm p.a.
4 the driest place in the world?	The Atacama Desert, Chile	<0.01 cm p.a.
5 the hottest place in the world?	El Azizia, Libya	57.8°C
6 the coldest place in the world?	The South Pole	-89.4°C
7 the largest desert in the world?	The Sahara	8.5 million km²
8 the largest ocean in the world?	The Pacific	166 million km²
9 the largest island in the world?	Australia	7.6 million km²
10 the largest lake in the world?	The Caspian Sea, Iran	371,000 km²
11 the longest mountain range?	The Andes, South America	7,200 km
12 the highest mountain in the world?	Mount Everest	8,848 m
13 the longest river in the world?	The Nile	6,670 km
14 the biggest river in the world?	The Amazon	delta = 7 million km²
15 the lowest point in the world?	The Dead Sea, Jordan	-395 metres

Language and culture note

There are three ways of referring to the body of water which stretches from Kuwait to the Straits of Hormuz. In American English, it is most commonly called the Persian Gulf. In British English, it is the Arabian Gulf or the Gulf. Allow your students to use whichever designation they are familiar with.

Closure

Drill the green words for pronunciation, especially stress.

Lesson 2: Speaking

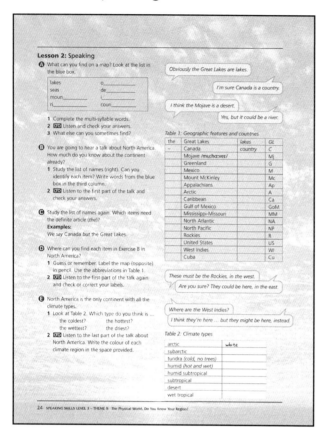

Introduction

Remind students of the green words from Lesson 1. Check pronunciation, perhaps with a quiz, e.g.,

Which words have …?

at least one schwa	*delta, desert, ocean, tropical*
have a /ʃ/ sound	*ocean*
have an /ɑː/ sound	*Arctic; Antarctic*
have an /əʊ/ sound	*ocean, pole*
have an /ɒ/ sound	*tropics, tropical*
have an /eɪ/ sound	*range*

You can allow the students to look at the words, since it is sound–sight that you are trying to reinforce with this exercise.

Work also on the clusters and suppressed plosives in all these words: *delta, range, Antarctic, Arctic, tropics, tropical.*

Ask students to draw a mountain range, a desert, an island, a delta and a lake.

Exercise A

Ask *What can you find on a map?* but do not allow students to answer. Refer them to the blue box.
1 Set for pairwork. Do not feed back.
2 Play the recording for students to check. Feed back orally. Note the appearance of schwa in a lot of these words. Drill for pronunciation.
3 Elicit ideas from the whole class and write them on the board.

Answers
3 Possible features are:
cities
borders
roads / railway lines + bridges
ferry routes
climate
hills / height marking

Exercise B

Make sure students understand why they are doing this activity – to prepare them for the listening, which in turn gives them a model for the speaking activity in Lesson 4.

Refer students to the map of North America on page 25 so they know what you are talking about.

Work through the first item as an example. Show how they can use the dialogue examples. Check the pronunciation of *Mojave.*
1 Set for pairwork. Monitor to get an idea of what students know already. Do not feed back. Tell them not to worry about the last column at this point.
2 Play the first part of the talk. Point out that on this hearing they only have to listen to check their ideas about each item, e.g., *The Mojave is a desert.*

Answers

Great Lakes	*lakes*
Canada	*country*
Mojave /muːhɑːveɪ/	desert
Greenland	country
Mexico	country
Mount McKinley	mountain
Appalachians	mountains
Arctic	ocean
Caribbean	sea
Gulf of Mexico	sea
Mississippi-Missouri	river
North Atlantic	ocean
North Pacific	ocean
Rockies	mountains
United States	country
West Indies	islands
Cuba	island and country

Exercise C

Set for pairwork. Feed back orally, but do not confirm or correct. Hopefully, students will now be sensitised to the issue and will notice more in the next hearing.

Methodology note

This is deep-end strategy. Can the students work out the use of the definite article with proper nouns from geography from the examples so far? It does not matter if they can't. The point is covered fully in Lesson 3.

Exercise D

1   Set for pairwork. Refer students to the speech bubbles. Drill. Explain the use of the abbreviations. Make sure students use pencils. Do not feed back.
2   Play the first part of the simplified version again. Feed back, ideally onto an OHT of the outline map.

Answers

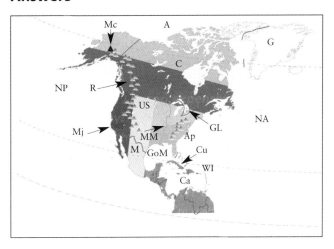

Exercise E

Remind students about the main elements of climate – temperature and rainfall. Refer students to the map, in particular the colouring. Explain that this shows the climate types. Refer students to Table 2.

1   Set the questions for pairwork. Only give a few seconds. It is an orientation activity. Monitor. Feed back on ideas, but do not confirm or correct.
2   Make sure students know how to refer to the different colours, i.e., *light / dark*. Set for individual work then pairwork checking. Play the second part of the simplified version. Feed back, ideally onto an OHT of the climate map.

Answers

Arctic	*white*
Subarctic	light blue
Tundra (*cold, no trees*)	dark blue
Humid (*hot and wet*)	light green
Humid subtropical	yellow
Subtropical	orange
Desert	red
Wet tropical	dark green

Closure

Test the students on the information on the North America map.

Lesson 3: Learning new skills

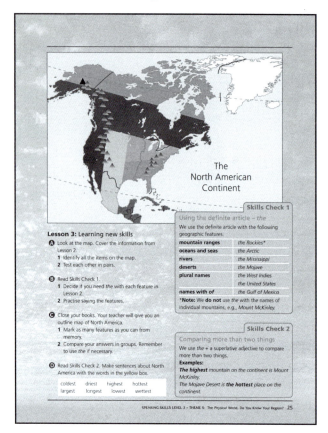

What is the name of the ● near the West Indies?
Where are the Rocky Mountains?
What's the name of the ocean north of Canada?

Exercise B

Refer students to the first table of information in
Lesson 2 and then Skills Check 1. Remind students
that they did this as a deep-end strategy, but now they
have some rules to apply.

1   Set for individual work then pairwork checking.
2   Drill, noting the intrusive sounds as applicable.

Answers

the?	item	reason
the	Great Lakes	it's a plural region
✗	Canada	it's a country
the	Mojave	it's a desert
✗	Greenland	it's a country
✗	Mexico	it's a country
✗	Mount McKinley	it's a mountain
the	/j/ Appalachians	it's a mountain range
the	/j/ Arctic	it's an ocean
the	Caribbean	it's a sea
the	Gulf of Mexico	it has the word *of*
the	Mississippi-Missouri	it's a river
the	North Atlantic	it's an ocean
the	North Pacific	it's an ocean
the	Rockies	it's a mountain range
the	/j/ United States	it's a plural country name
the	West Indies	it's a plural region
✗	Cuba	it's a country

Introduction

Practise saying some or all of the words from the two
tables in Lesson 2. Concentrate on stress and making
an English-sounding word; many of these words will
be similar in the students' own languages, but
pronounced differently.

Note: Assuming the students completed Lesson 2
correctly, the maps in their books should be covered with
abbreviations. If there are some students who were not
present at the previous lesson, put them in a pair with
a student who has the abbreviations in his / her book.

Exercise A

1   Set for pairwork. Feed back, checking all the
    abbreviations.
2   Set for pairwork. Give some structures for students
    to use when they test each other, e.g.,

Exercise C

1   Give out the outline map of North America (page
    72 of this book). Set for individual work.
2   Pairwork checking.

Exercise D

Remind students about the rules for making superlatives.

Refer students to the information about climate – the colour coding and the key that they completed in Lesson 2. Point out that in many cases they are guessing the answers.

Feed back, explaining that they will hear the correct information in the next lesson.

Methodology note

Don't worry about spelling rules. This is a Speaking course. The use of *the* and saying the consonant cluster *st* at the end of the form is much more important.

Closure

Ask students about their own countries or regions – the hottest area, wettest area, etc.

Set the research task for Lesson 4 – finding out information about students' own continent / region.

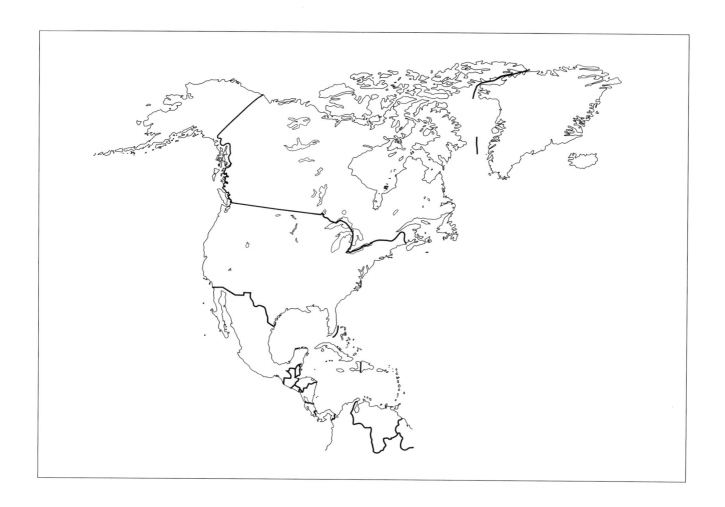

Lesson 4: Applying new skills

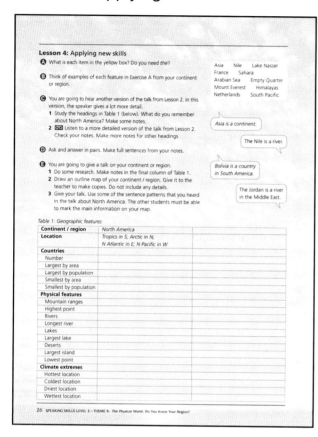

Introduction

Go through a list of geographic features, asking students to name items until they run out (as shown below). Check that they are using *the* as appropriate.

- continents
- countries
- mountain ranges
- mountains
- oceans
- seas
- rivers
- deserts
- lakes
- islands

Note: The region *the Middle East* probably requires the definite article because it is derived from *the East*. We normally use the definite article with points of the compass.

Exercise A

Set for individual work then pairwork checking. Refer students to the first pair of speech bubbles. Feed back orally.

Answers
Asia
the Nile
France
Lake Nasser
Mount Everest
the Arabian Sea
the Empty Quarter
the Himalayas
the Netherlands
the Sahara
the South Pacific

Exercise B

Set for pairwork. Refer students to the second pair of speech bubbles. Feed back orally.

Exercise C

Refer students to Table 1. Point out that we often do not use the definite article in notes, but we must say it. Remind students how to abbreviate units of measurement – square kilometres, centimetres, metres, kilometres, degrees centigrade (including minus).

1 Set for pairwork. Do not feed back.
2 Play the recording. Give plenty of time for completing the notes. Feed back onto the board or onto an OHT.

Answers

Model notes

Continent / region	North America
Location	*Tropics in S; Arctic in N; N. Atlantic in E; N. Pacific in W*
Countries Number Largest by area Largest by population Smallest by area Smallest by population	24, inc. Mexico and Cuba Canada = 10 m km² (US = >9 m km²) US = >250 m St Kitts and Nevis = 269 km² St Kitts and Nevis = 38 k
Physical features Mountain ranges Highest point Rivers Longest river Lakes Largest lake Deserts Largest island Lowest point	Appalachians, Rockies Mount McKinley = 6,000 m St Lawrence, Colorado Mississippi-Missouri, = 4,000 km The Great Lakes Lake Superior = 80,000 km² Mojave Greenland = >2 m km² Death Valley = -86 metres
Climate extremes Hottest location Coldest location Driest location Wettest location	Death Valley (Mojave) = 50°C Greenland = -70°C Death Valley = 4 cm p.a. NW US = 400 cm p.a.

Exercise D

Set for pairwork. Monitor. Feed back by getting some of the students to demonstrate parts of their conversations.

Exercise E

If possible, be prepared to take in maps and copy them during this phase of the lesson.

If students are all from the same country, they can obviously compete to give the best talk. Otherwise, it becomes a genuine information transfer activity. Consider putting students from different countries into continent groups to prepare the notes.

Take notes of general points during the talks.

Closure

Feed back on general points.

Lesson 1: Vocabulary

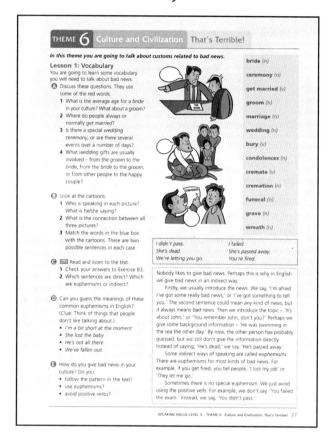

Linking – C + V: carrying sound of final consonant on to beginning of the next word

Linking – V + V: with intrusive /j/, /r/ and /w/

Linking – suppressed consonants: e.g., *I go(t) the job*

Shifting word stress: e.g., *'hibernate – hiber'nation*

Introduction

Note: On this occasion, the green words, which are all connected with death, are not introduced in Lesson 1. Clearly the whole issue of talking about death is very sensitive, but it is essential that students are given the necessary vocabulary if they are going to operate in English in the future. The value of this lesson will certainly be clear to anyone who has been faced with an extremely sad situation in a foreign culture and suddenly realised that they do not have the vocabulary or cultural knowledge to deal with it.

If students did Level 2, they should be able to remember the red words. If not, spend a few minutes checking that they know the words. Perhaps set this as a group task, with one student looking up each word and reporting back on meaning and pronunciation, especially stress, to the other students in the group. Check pronunciation, especially the following points:

bride	initial cluster; diphthong
ceremony	pronunciation of *c*; schwa for *o*
married	stress; final short vowel
marriage	stress; final short vowel, pron of *g*
groom	initial cluster

Exercise A

Set for group work. If students are from different cultures, put people from different cultures into each group. Feed back orally.

In the course to date, students have studied the following areas of spoken English and phonology. Take every opportunity to practise these points further in this theme. In particular, whenever students are reading text aloud or doing pairwork, monitor and note failure to link sounds in an English way.

Speaking skills

Stating sources – *According to …*

Talking about importance and relevance – *It's not important how good his work is.*

Indicating partial comprehension – *I don't understand the part about …*

Using the definite article with proper nouns – *The Himalayas* but *Mount Everest*

Comparing more than two things – *the biggest lake in the world*

Phonology

Making yourself clear – minimal pairs with vowel, consonant and stress changes

Exercise B

Refer students to the cartoons.

1 Elicit ideas about the situations and what the people are saying. Give students useful vocabulary like *boss* and *vet*, but do not confirm or correct the actual words – the students check for themselves in the next exercise.

2 Elicit the connection between the cartoons – bad news. Elicit other examples of bad news, including, if students are prepared to mention it, death in the family or terminal disease. Do not introduce the topic if students do not bring it up.

3 Set for pairwork. Elicit ideas, but still do not confirm or correct.

Exercise C

1 Set for individual work then pairwork checking. Play the recording. Feed back, eliciting ideas and finally confirming and correcting.

2 Build up the answer table on the board. Drill the pronunciation of the key word *euphemism* = /'juːfəmɪzm/.

Answers

	Direct statement	Euphemism or indirect statement
1	*You're fired.*	*We're letting you go.*
2	*She's dead.*	*She's passed away.*
3	*I failed.*	*I didn't pass.*

Methodology note

This is a Speaking skills lesson, so why have a long text for listening and reading? In order to produce new spoken language and monitor one's own production, we need many good models. Aural learners need to actually hear these models, visual learners need to actually see these models. This exercise ensures that both types of learners are accommodated. In addition, giving students a chance to listen while they read reinforces sight–sound relationships, which are so important to good pronunciation.

Exercise D

Set for pairwork. Feed back orally. Confirm or correct.

Answers
I'm a bit short at the moment.
I haven't got much / any money.

She lost the baby.
The baby died before it was born.

He's not all there.
He has mental problems.

We've fallen out.
We have had an argument.

Exercise E

This could be quite an interesting discussion, if the students get into it. Does the same pattern exist in other languages, i.e.,

introduce the fact of bad news;
introduce the topic;
give some background information;
give the news in an indirect way?

Is the use of euphemism a universal trait, or are some cultures / speech communities prepared to be completely direct in giving bad news or talking about 'taboo' subjects?

Closure

1   Check comprehension of the text in Exercise C in more detail, perhaps by reading the text again, students' books closed, with mistakes, e.g.,

Everybody likes to give bad news. Perhaps this is why in English we give bad *newspapers* in a *direct* way.

Firstly, we usually introduce the news. We say, '*I'm happy I've got some really good news,*' or '*I've got nothing bad to tell you.*' The second sentence could mean **any** kind of news, but it *never* means **bad** news. Then we introduce *a friend* – 'It's about John,' or 'You *forget* John, don't you?' Perhaps we give some background *stories* – 'He was *running* in the sea *tomorrow*.' By now, the other person has probably guessed, but we still don't give the information *indirectly*. Instead of saying, 'He's dead,' we say 'He's passed *his exam*.'

Some indirect ways of speaking are called *you for me*. There are euphemisms for most kinds of bad news. For example, if you get fired, you say to people, '*I lost my work*' or '*They allowed me to go.*'

Sometimes there is no special euphemism. We just avoid using the positive verb. For example, we don't say, 'You failed the exam.' Instead, we say, '*You didn't fail.*'

2   Ask students to think of negative phrases with the same meaning as the positive verbs below.

lost	didn't win
failed	didn't pass
died	didn't survive
argued	didn't get on
rejected	didn't accept

Lesson 2: Speaking

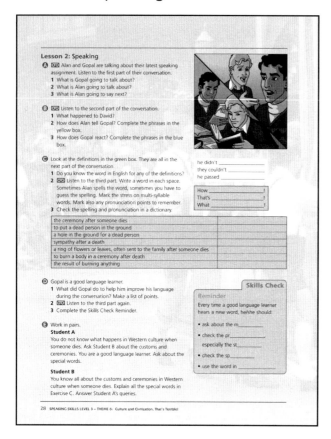

Answers

1 His country and another country.
2 He hasn't decided.
3 He is going to give Gopal some bad news.

Exercise B

Set for pairwork. Play Part 2. Feed back orally. Drill the reaction phrases. Highlight the difference between the phrases with adjectives and the one with a noun. Tell the students some more bad news – invent it! Ask them to react.

Answers

1 He was killed in a road accident.
2 He says:
   he didn't *make it*
   they couldn't *save him*
   he passed *away*
3 He says:
   How *awful*! = adjective phrase
   That's *terrible*! = adjective phrase
   What *a dreadful thing to happen*! = noun phrase

Exercise C

Explain that words for all the definitions appear in the next part of the conversation.

1 Give students a few moments to look at the definitions – they may know one or two of the words, but do not confirm or correct
2 Set for individual work then pairwork checking. Play Part 3. Give students time to work out the words, spellings, etc., in pairs.
3 Set for pairwork. Feed back onto the board.

Introduction

Refer students to the illustration. Ask for ideas on what is happening. Give names to the characters – Alan from England and Gopal from India. Ask what they are doing in the first picture and what has happened in the second picture. Elicit ideas on what Alan is saying to Gopal and what he is replying. Students should be able to see that Alan is giving Gopal bad news (they have been primed for this by Lesson 1, of course). Confirm this, but do not confirm or correct any other points. Note, however, whether students are able to react to bad news.

Exercise A

Set for pairwork. Play Part 1. Feed back orally. Point out particularly the expression *By the way*, which changes the subject, and then the introduction of bad news.

Answers

definition	word	pronunciation points
the ceremony after someone dies	'funeral	schwa
to put a dead person in the ground	'bury	always check pronunciation of 'ur'; cf. *hurry* /ʌr/; *fury* /juːr/; *fur* /ɜː/
the hole in the ground for a dead person	grave	*diphthong*
sympathy after a death	con'dolences	*schwa on first syllable; schwa on third syllable*
a ring of flowers or leaves, often sent to the family after someone dies	wreath	*silent w*
to burn a body in a ceremony after death	cremate	*first e = /ɪ/; diphthong /eɪ/*
the result of burning anything	ashes	

Exercise D

Elicit some ideas about the behaviour of good language learners. If students did Level 2, they should be able to do this well. Even if they did not, they can brainstorm some points. Do not refer to the Skills Check at this point.

1   Set for individual work then pairwork checking. Play Part 3 again. Do not feed back.
2   Set for pairwork. Feed back, building up the list on the board.

Add an extra rule for good language learning, as follows:

a   Point to the word *cremate*. Elicit the fact that it is a verb.
b   Ask students to guess the noun. If they hesitate, point out that multi-syllable nouns often end in *-ence / -ance*, *-tion*, *-ment* or *-ness*. However, *-ness* is only added to an adjective, e.g., *happiness*, *sadness*, *loveliness*. The ending *-tion* is the most common when building from a verb that ends in *e*, especially *te*. Therefore, the most likely noun is *cremation*.
c   Where is the stress? Remind students of the 80% rule (studied in Theme 4) and the exception with nouns ending in *-tion*: because the final two syllables have become one. Q.E.D.: The stress is probably on the vowel before *-tion*.

d   What should they do now? Check in a dictionary. So what is the extra rule for good language learning? *Look at the new word and try to build other words from it – or link it to other words you already know. Check your ideas with a dictionary.*

Answers

Every time a good language learner hears a new word, he / she should:
*   ask about the meaning;
*   check the pronunciation, especially the stress;
*   check the spelling;
*   use the word in the next sentence (and ten times in the next week, according to the Skills Check in Level 2).

Exercise E

Set up the role play. Monitor and assist. Get some pairs to demonstrate parts of their conversation in front of the class.

Closure

Play the part of a person who doesn't know Western culture. Use a lot of tag questions as a preview of the Skills Checks in the next lesson, e.g., *They send wreaths in Western culture, don't they? A wreath is a ring of flowers or leaves, isn't it?*

Lesson 3: Learning new skills

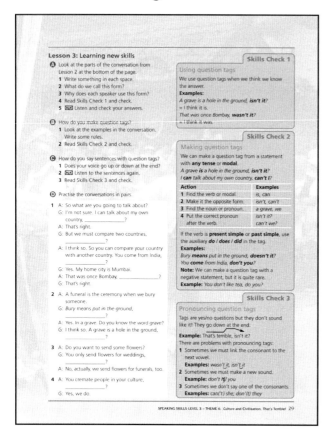

Introduction

Remind students of the green words (listed in Lesson 1 but presented in Lesson 2 on this occasion). They can look at the words as they try to answer the questions. This reinforces sound–sight relationships. Check pronunciation, perhaps with a quiz, e.g.,

Which words have …?

at least one schwa	*condolence*; *funeral* + possibly *cremate*, *cremation* – see note below
a silent letter	*(w)reath*
an /e/ sound	*bury*
an /ɪ/ sound	*cremate*, *cremation* – note: some English speakers may use a schwa for the first vowel
an /iː/ sound	*wreath*
a /əʊ/ sound	*condolences*
an /uː/ sound	*funeral* – note full sound = /juː/
an /eɪ/ sound	*grave*, *cremate*, *cremation*
a /ʃ/ sound	*cremation*
a /θ/ sound	*wreath*

Work also on the clusters and suppressed consonants in:

condolences, cremate, cremation, funeral, grave

Exercise A

1   Set for individual work then pairwork checking. Do not feed back.
2–4 Set for pairwork. Do not feed back.
5   Play the recording. Feed back, ideally onto an OHT of the extracts.

Answers

1   Answers depend on students.
2   Question tag.
3   Because he thinks he knows the answer – he thinks his statement is true.
5   Target words in italics.

A: So what are you going to talk about?
G: I'm not sure. I can talk about my own country, *can't I*?
A: That's right.
G: But we must compare two countries, *mustn't we*?
A: I think so. So you can compare your country with another country. You come from India, *don't you*?
G: Yes. My home city is Mumbai.
A: That was once Bombay, *wasn't it*?
G: That's right.

A: A funeral is the ceremony when we bury someone.
G: **Bury** means put in the ground, *doesn't it*?
A: Yes. In a grave. Do you know the word **grave**?
G: I think so. A grave is a hole in the ground, *isn't it*?

A: Do you want to send some flowers?

G: You only send flowers for weddings, *don't you?*

A: No, actually, we send flowers for funerals, too.

A: You cremate people in your culture, *don't you?*

G: Yes, we do.

Exercise B

Set for pairwork. Feed back onto the board after students have had a chance to read Skills Check 2 and check their rules. Go through the rules carefully with several examples.

Answers
See Skills Check 2.

Methodology note

If you wish, extend the use of question tags to the following case – not in the conversation as recorded:

> Gopal: *Send the family my condolences, won't you?*
>
> Alan: *Yes, I will.*

Point out that the imperative in this case really means *You will do this for me,* so the tag uses *will* and so does the response, *Yes, I will.*

Exercise C

1 Set for individual work then pairwork checking. Do not feed back.
2 Play the recording again.
3 Set for individual work then pairwork checking. Feed back, showing the intonation pattern then drilling it. Drill also the linking points with examples.

Answers
See Skills Check 3.

Methodology note

According to corpus research, tags based on positive statements are four times as common in conversation as tags based on negative statements. For this reason, I do not muddy the waters with the *negative statement to positive tag* possibility. Nor do I introduce the alternative tag pronunciation, in which you are unsure of the answer. This is too complex for this level.

Incidentally, tags are extremely rare in fiction and unknown in academic text.

Exercise D

Set for pairwork. Monitor and assist with intonation and linking.

Closure

Check information that you believe is true about students in the class with question tags. Talk about the past and the future, if possible.

Invite students to check information that they believe is true about you. Encourage them to check past and future points. If students don't know you very well, give them a series of facts about yourself (present, past and future) and then get students to try and remember and check them.

Methodology note

If you have taught this class for some time, they *should* know a lot about you. Remember! A good teacher talks about him / herself. (Not all the time, of course.)

Lesson 4: Applying new skills

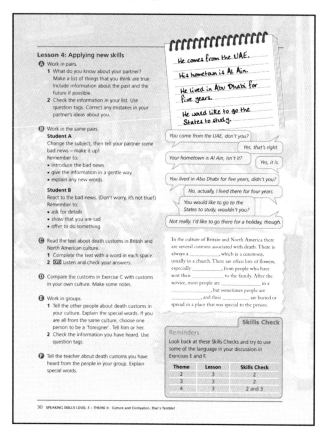

Introduction

Remind students about the exercise at the end of the previous lesson – when they checked information about you. Repeat the activity for a few moments.

Exercise A

1 Refer students to the examples. Work through them. Point out that one is about the past and one about the future. Set for individual work.
2 Refer students to the speech bubbles. Work through the examples. Set for pairwork. Monitor and assist. End with some pairs demonstrating particularly good checking sentences. Point out the examples where the information is, in fact, wrong and must be corrected, gently of course in order not to offend.

Exercise B

Remind students of the typical structure of giving bad news. Build up a table on the board.

Action	Example / exponent
Change the subject – if you were talking about something else before.	*By the way ... / Oh, I forgot to say ...*
Introduce the bad news.	*I've got something to tell you. / I'm afraid I've got some (really) bad / terrible news.*
Give the topic.	*It's about John.*
Give some background information. This allows the person to guess the bad news. We probably ought to come straight out and say it, but we often don't. Note the use of the past continuous in this situation. Note also that we sometimes give the euphemism first, then this kind of detail.	*He was swimming in the sea the other day.*
Give the news, with euphemisms or indirect statements.	*He's passed away.*

Remind students also of the way the other person can ask for information ...

What happened? How did it happen?

... and how they can react. Build up a table on the board:

How	awful	
That's	terrible	*!*
What a (n)	dreadful	*thing to happen!*

Set for pairwork. Monitor and assist. Get some of the best pairs to demonstrate.

Exercise C

Remind students that they heard about death customs in the West in Lesson 2, and learnt some special words.
1   Set for individual work then pairwork checking. Tell students not to worry too much about spelling.
2   Play the recording. Feed back, ideally onto an OHT of the text.

Answers

Target words in italics
In the culture of Britain and North America there are several customs associated with death. There is always a *funeral*, which is a ceremony, usually in a church. There are often lots of flowers, especially *wreaths*, from people who have sent their *condolences* to the family. After the service, most people are *buried* in a *grave*, but sometimes people are *cremated*, and their *ashes* are buried or spread in a place that was special to the person.

Exercise D

Set for individual work and pairwork checking, if students are all from the same culture, OR put students into pairs or groups from the same culture. Monitor and assist. Get students to explain any special words to you. Pretend ignorance of even common words like *mosque / temple*.

Exercise E

1   Follow the instructions.
2   Remind students about using question tags.

Exercise F

Refer students to the Skills Check Reminders and give them time to look up the references.

Follow the instructions. Try to confirm the information you have understood with question tags. Make some mistakes so students have to correct you, gently of course.

Closure

Ask the students to do some research into death customs in other cultures and report back, stating their sources as in Theme 2 Lesson 3 Skills Check 3 (if they are Internet / printed materials) or using the phrases for talking about something they have heard (if they have got the information from friends from different cultures).

Lesson 1: Vocabulary

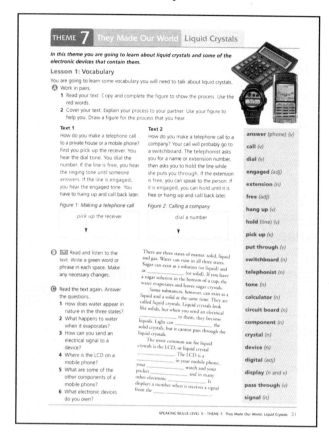

Introduction

Refer students to the illustration of a mobile phone. Check / teach the name. Note that the students may prefer to call it a *cell phone* (US English). Hold up your own mobile or borrow one from a student. Ask what makes it work. Elicit *battery.*

If students did Level 2, remind them about speaking on the telephone in English. Otherwise explain that there is a lot of special telephone language in English.

Exercise A

Set for pairwork. Monitor and assist. Feed back by building up the model figures on the board. Drill the red words. Leave on the board and return to this later.

Answers

Model figures

Figure 1: Making a telephone call

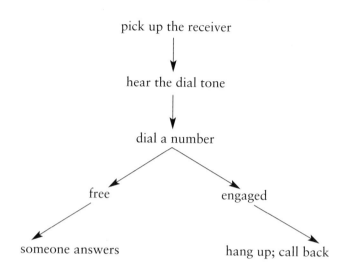

Figure 2: Calling a company

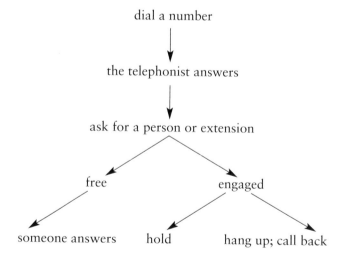

Exercise B

Set for individual work then pairwork checking. Play the recording. Feed back orally. Do not ask comprehension questions at this point – the next exercise checks comprehension.

Answers

Target words in italics

There are three states of matter: solid, liquid and gas. Water can exist in all three states. Sugar can exist as a solution (or liquid) and as *crystals* (or solid). If you leave a sugar solution in the bottom of a cup, the water evaporates and leaves sugar crystals.

Some substances, however, can exist as a liquid and a solid at the same time. They are called liquid crystals. Liquid crystals look like solids, but when you send an electrical *signal* to them, they become liquids. Light can *pass through* the solid crystals, but it cannot pass through the liquid crystals.

The most common use for liquid crystals is the LCD, or liquid crystal *display*. The LCD is a *component* in your mobile phone, your *digital* watch and your pocket *calculator* and in many other electronic *devices*. It displays a number when it receives a signal from the *circuit board*.

Exercise C

Set for pairwork. Monitor and assist. Feed back orally, eliciting as much of the detail in the Answers below as possible. Check comprehension of the text, particularly the idea that:

> When you send an electrical signal to a liquid crystal, it becomes a liquid. Light *cannot pass through* the liquid crystals.

It is vital that students understand this point for the next lesson.

Answers

1   solid = hail, ice, snow; liquid = rivers, seas, lakes, oceans, ponds, etc.; gas = steam, clouds
2   It changes from a liquid to a gas.
3   Through a wire, or more exactly, by connecting it to a power source and closing a switch – draw a simple circuit on the board (see next lesson).

4   It is on the screen or display.
5   Answers depend on students, but they should remember *battery* and might be able to say *keys* or *key pad*, *screen* and *SIM card*.
6   Answers depend on students, but elicit as many as possible.

Methodology note

Students who did Speaking Level 2 Theme 4 will be familiar with the idea of states of matter – you will need to go more slowly over these points with other students.

Closure

Erase some of the key words from the two figures on making a phone call (from Exercise A). Elicit the words.

Role-play a conversation with a telephonist. See if students can work out what to say and do in response to your statements as the telephonist. Then swap roles with a bright student. Finally set for pairwork based on Figure 2.

Lesson 2: Speaking

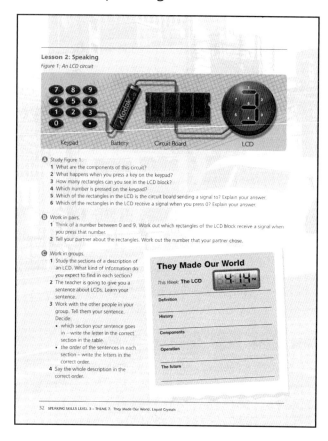

Introduction

Test students on the pronunciation of the green words from Lesson 1, as follows:

Which multi-syllable words are stressed on:

the first syllable?	*calculator, circuit, crystal, digital, signal*
the second syllable?	*component, device, display*

Which word(s) has / have:

schwa?	*calculator, component, crystal, digital, signal* – point out that the ending *al* is normally pronounced with a schwa
/ɪ/?	*circu**i**t, cr**y**stal, d**e**vice, dig**i**tal, displ**ay**, s**i**gnal* – note that some of these are quite surprising
/dʒ/?	*digital*
/k/?	*calculator, circuit, component, crystal*

/r/? only *crystal*, and *through* – in the other words with *r* the sound is not made (viz *calculator, circuit, board*)

Drill the clusters in *calculator, component, crystal, display, signal, through*.

Remember that students can look at the words as they answer the questions, as you are trying to reinforce the sound–sight relationships.

Note: Some students may notice the use of the indefinite article *an* in front of a consonant *L* in the title of the figure (i.e., *An LCD circuit*). If so, point out that the use of *an* is based on the sound of the following letter, not whether the letter is a vowel or a consonant. This might come as quite a shock to some students! Give further examples, e.g.,

an F111 (one eleven) – an American jet fighter
an SUV – a sports utility vehicle, e.g., a jeep or similar
an MP – a member of parliament
an Ngage mobile phone
an X-ray

Some people say *an hotel* because they do not pronounce the *h*, although this is old-fashioned now.

Note, conversely (because the initial sound is /j/):
a European country
a university campus

Exercise A

Write the key sentences from the Lesson 1 text on the board again, as follows:

When you send an electrical signal to a liquid crystal, it becomes a liquid. Light cannot pass through the liquid crystals.

Gradually erase words while students try to remember and say the sentences. In the end, everything except the first word of each sentence should be erased, but students should still be able to say the sentences.

Set for pairwork. Feed back, ideally onto an OHT of the circuit. Show how pressing the key 3 sends a signal to rectangles 5 and 7 so light cannot pass through.

Answers

1 An LCD, a circuit board, a battery and a key pad. **Note:** There is also wire, but it is not a component.
2 It sends a signal to the circuit board, which sends a signal to the LCD.
3 7
4 3
5 #5 and 7 – those rectangles are not letting light pass through.
6 #6 – because this is the only one that you don't want light to pass through.

Exercise B

Set for pairwork. Monitor and assist. Feed back, eliciting and building up a table for all the numbers. Encourage different students to explain exactly what is happening for each number. Check and correct pronunciation and grammar.

Answers

No.	signal to rectangle:							notes
	1	2	3	4	5	6	7	
0						✓		
1	✓		✓	✓	✓		✓	if on right side
2		✓				✓		
3				✓		✓		
4	✓			✓	✓			show the possible shape of this number
5		✓			✓			
6		✓						
7			✓	✓	✓	✓		
8								no signals sent because the rectangles = 8!
9				✓				

Exercise C

Explain that in this theme the students are going to learn to give a description of a device. Put students in groups of 7 or 14. If this is not possible, simply divide the class into three groups.

1 Point out that descriptions of devices often have the sections in the table. Pre-teach the word *operation* = how something works. Elicit ideas for content in each case. Do not confirm or correct.
2 Make copies of the lettered jigsaw sentences on page 92 and cut them up. Give each student in a group one or more of the sentences. Explain that students must learn their sentence(s). They will be allowed to refer back to it later, but they will not be allowed to read it out.
3 Follow the instructions as written.
4 Follow the instructions as written.

Feed back, ideally revealing an OHT of the model version.

Methodology note

Any activity that forces students to memorise a text is likely to improve language learning. You can keep something with no meaning – like a random set of words – in short-term memory for a few seconds, but unless you can turn something meaningless into something meaningful, you cannot transfer it to long-term memory (which simply means you can't remember it). So even if a sentence in this exercise is meaningless when a student first reads it, he / she must make some sense of it to remember it later.

There is a second advantage to this kind of memory exercise. The brain needs many examples of good language use in order to make (subconscious) hypotheses about language structure. The more examples you give the brain, the better it can do its work. It is not just chance that gets young children to memorise stories, songs and poems in their first language.

Answers

The most logical structure of the text is printed in 15-point type on page 91 for you to make an OHT.

Closure

Focus on some of the structural points in the sentences. This works particularly well if you have been able to display the completed text on an OHT. You only need to spend a few minutes on this, however, as it is fully exploited in the next lesson.

Definition	f	An LCD, or liquid-crystal display, is an electronic device.
	c	It is used for displaying numbers and, sometimes, letters.
History	i	Liquid crystals were first discovered in 1888 by an Austrian botanist called Friedrich Reinitzer.
	e	However, it was 80 years before the American company RCA made the first LCD in 1968.
	n	Nowadays there are LCDs in most modern electronic devices, such as mobile telephones, pocket calculators and digital watches.
Components	b	An LCD consists of a light source and a number of liquid crystals.
	m	The crystals are usually arranged into blocks of seven rectangles that form the number 8 in English.
Operation	j	Each block of rectangles receives electrical signals from the circuit board.
	a	The electricity changes the crystals in some rectangles from solid to liquid.
	h	These crystals become liquid and light cannot pass through these rectangles.
	d	The number is displayed by the rectangles that are still solid.
The future	l	LCDs will probably replace cathode-ray tubes (or CRTs) in large television screens.
	k	They will probably also be used to make cameras the size of credit cards.
	g	They may even be made into electronic notebooks that can display data and 'read' handwriting.

a	The electricity changes the crystals in some rectangles from solid to liquid.
b	An LCD consists of a light source and a number of liquid crystals.
c	It is used for displaying numbers and, sometimes, letters.
d	The number is displayed by the rectangles that are still solid.
e	However, it was 80 years before the American company RCA made the first LCD in 1968.
f	An LCD, or liquid-crystal display, is an electronic device.
g	They may even be made into electronic notebooks that can display data and 'read' handwriting.
h	These crystals become liquid and light cannot pass through these rectangles.
i	Liquid crystals were first discovered in 1888 by an Austrian botanist called Friedrich Reinitzer.
j	Each block of rectangles receives electrical signals from the circuit board.
k	They will probably also be used to make cameras the size of credit cards.
l	LCDs will probably replace cathode-ray tubes (or CRTs) in large television screens.
m	The crystals are usually arranged into blocks of seven rectangles that form the number 8 in English.
n	Nowadays there are LCDs in most modern electronic devices, such as mobile telephones, pocket calculators and digital watches.

Lesson 3: Learning new skills

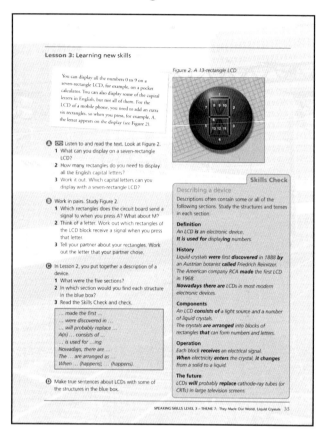

Introduction

Ask students to remember a word from this theme with the following sounds – they are all the stressed syllables from the green words.

stressed syllable	word
cal	'calculator
cir	'circuit board
po	com'ponent
crys	'crystal
vice	de'vice
di	'digital
play	dis'play
sig	'signal

Drill the words.

Exercise A

Set for individual work then pairwork checking. Play the recording. Feed back orally, taking time to make sure the key points are understood – see the notes in the Answers.

Answers

1　All the numbers 0 – 9.

2　Thirteen – note even with this number, V is strange, with a cross-piece and a right-hand vertical.

3　A B C D (but it looks like O) E F G H I J L O (but it looks like D) P S U. You cannot display K M N Q R T V W X Y Z.

Exercise B

1　Set for pairwork. Feed back orally. Get some groups to give their answers and produce a model sentence on the board, as follows:

> *When you press the letter A, the circuit board sends electrical signals to rectangles 4, 8, 9, 10, 11, 12 and 13.*

Repeat for M.

2 and 3 Monitor and assist. Feed back by getting some groups to give their sentences using the model on the board.

Answers

1　A = signals to 4, 8, 9, 10, 11, 12, 13; M = 1, 4, 6, 9, 11, 12, 13.

2 and 3 Answers depend on students, but the rectangles that receive signals must be the ones that light does <u>not</u> pass through.

Exercise C

1 Ask students to cover the Skills Check in the right-hand column. Elicit the five sections. Check pronunciation.
2 Elicit some answers then set for pairwork. Monitor and assist. Do not feed back.
3 Set for individual work then pairwork checking. Feed back, ideally with an OHT copy of the Skills Check. Highlight key structural points.

Answers

1 Definition, History, Components, Operation, The future
2 See Skills Check.

Exercise D

Set for pairwork. Feed back orally.

Closure

Give the facts about LCDs, but make mistakes of content, not form, for pupils to correct, e.g., An LCD, or *light*-crystal display, is used for *writing* numbers and letters.

Liquid crystals were first discovered in *1988* by an *Australian* botanist called Friedrich Reinitzer.

Lesson 4: Applying new skills

device it is. They cannot ask about function unless they are completely stuck, e.g.,

> *What can you see on the LCD?*
> *What is the power source? / How is it powered?*
> *What are some of the components?*

To make it even harder, say that they can only ask *Yes / No* questions, e.g.,

> *Can you see numbers on the LCD?*
> *Is there a keypad?*

Answers

See the table on page 97 of this book.

Exercise B

This is practice for the *Operation* section of the final activity in this lesson. Remind students of the key sentences from the *Operation* section of the Skills Check in Lesson 3. Describe the operation of one of the devices yourself, then get students to describe it. Set for pairwork. Students work out a description in pairs. Monitor. Feed back by getting students to say some of the better descriptions.

Exercise C

This is practice for the *Future* section of the final activity in this lesson. Set for pairwork. Feed back orally.

Exercise D

Follow the instructions as written. Photocopy and give out the texts on pages 99–101 or refer students to the relevant place in their Course Books, as follows:

> Watch = page 59
> Calculator = page 60
> Mobile = page 61

There is also a full-page copy of the blank table on page 98 of this book if you want to use it as a handout.

Closure

Students read the other two texts and compare the information with their notes. They discuss with the other people in the group why there are discrepancies.

Introduction

Refer students to the illustrations and get them to say what the devices are. Drill the pronunciation. If you feel up to it, get students to close their books, mime each item and elicit the name. Alternatively, point to all or some of the items if they happen to be in the room.

Exercise A

The first part of the activity is practice for the *Definition* section of the final activity in this lesson. The fourth part is practice for the *Components* section.

Set each part as teacher-paced pairwork. Feed back on each section, building up the table in the Answers (below) on the board.

If you think there will be time, set up a guessing game. A student has to choose one of the devices, but not name it. Students can ask questions to work out which

device	function	LCDs*	power source	components*
CD drive	a device for playing music and multimedia computer programs	track numbers	mains, USB	tray, lights, laser, motor
laptop	a portable personal computer	icons	mains, rechargeable battery	keypad, screen, lights, CD drive
mobile phone	a portable telephone that transmits and receives signals from base stations	numbers, names, messages	rechargeable battery	keypad, screen, antenna
personal stereo	a portable device for playing music from CD or cassette	track numbers	battery	headphones, laser (with CD version), motor
photocopier	a device for making copies of paper documents	paper size, number of copies	mains	glass, lid, scanner, paper trays, keypad
pocket calculator	a portable device for performing arithmetical functions, such as adding and subtracting	numbers, functions = + −, etc.	battery, solar cell	keypad, screen
printer	a device for producing paper copies of computer (i.e., digital) documents	paper size, number of copies required / made	mains	paper tray, print cartridges, motor
scanner	a device for converting paper documents into computer (i.e., digital) documents	paper size	mains	glass, lid, scanner, keypad
videotape recorder	a device for recording and playing back television programmes	time, time to end of tape	mains	remote control, motor
watch	a portable device for measuring and displaying time	numbers, names = months	battery, perhaps self-charging, solar cell	quartz crystal, display

*The words in these columns are just examples. Students may not come up with these words or may produce other correct words. Do not push this. The aim is not to teach hundreds of component words, for example, just to reinforce the idea that *components* = the parts of a device.

	They Made Our World		
	watch	calculator	mobile
Definition			
History			
Components			
Operation			
The future			

	They Made Our World	A
	The Digital Quartz Watch	
Definition	A watch is a portable device for measuring and displaying time. A digital quartz watch is powered by a crystal of quartz and displays time as numbers.	
History	The first watches appeared shortly after 1500. In that year, Peter Henlein, a locksmith from Germany, invented the spring-powered watch. Until then, clocks needed large weights. There were many improvements to the watch in the next 400 years, but they still needed a spring that was wound by hand. In 1957, an American company, The Hamilton Watch Company, invented a battery-powered watch. The first quartz watch appeared on the market in 1969. It was made by the Japanese company Seiko, but it was not digital. It still had a face and hands like a traditional watch. Three years later, the Hamilton Watch Company brought out the Pulsar, the first digital quartz watch. Nowadays, digital watches are more popular than analogue with many people, particularly teenagers.	
Components	A digital quartz watch consists of a miniature battery, a thin slice of quartz, which is a kind of crystal rock, a circuit board and an LCD for numbers and letters. There are also buttons for changing the time.	
Operation	The battery provides electricity, which is applied to the quartz. The quartz vibrates 32,768 times each second. The microchip coverts this vibration into one signal per second. This signal is converted into electronic instruction to the LCD, which displays a set of numbers. The numbers show the correct time.	
The future	People will soon be able to buy a TV watch that has a liquid-crystal video display. The pictures are blue on a grey background. It will receive TV and radio signals.	

	They Made Our World **B**
	The Solar-powered Pocket Calculator
Definition	A pocket calculator is a portable device for performing arithmetical functions, such as adding and subtracting. A solar-powered calculator is powered by light, from the sun or other sources.
History	Blaise Pascal, a famous French mathematician, invented a digital arithmetic machine in 1642. Later in the 17th century, a German, Gottfried Leibniz, created a more advanced machine. Over the next 300 years, calculators became smaller and smaller. In 1974, the American Company, Texas Instruments, obtained a patent for a pocket electronic calculator. The calculator had a battery, a circuit board and a display with green numbers. Two years later, an LCD replaced the green display, and two years after that, in 1978, the first solar-powered calculator was produced by the Japanese company, Sharp. Calculators used to cost as much as a new car. Nowadays you can buy a solar-powered pocket calculator for the price of a beefburger.
Components	A solar-powered pocket calculator consists of a solar cell that converts light into electricity, a keypad with numbers and functions, such as add or subtract, a circuit board and an LCD for numbers. There is sometimes also a miniature battery to provide back-up power.
Operation	The main energy source is the solar cell. This provides electricity. When you press a key, a switch is closed and a signal is sent to the LCD. This signal is converted into electronic instruction to the LCD, which displays the number or the function. It is also stored in the memory section of the microchip. When you press the 'equals' key, the microchip does the calculation and the result is displayed on the LCD.
The future	Pocket calculators will probably store and display spreadsheets with many rows and columns of figures. They will probably communicate directly with personal computers.

	They Made Our World C
	The Mobile Phone
Definition	A telephone is a device for communicating with people over long distances through speech. A mobile phone is a portable telephone that transmits and receives signals from radio masts. A mobile phone is powered by a rechargeable battery.
History	In 1843, the British scientist, Michael Faraday, proved that the air could conduct electricity. Twenty years later, in 1865, Dr Loomis, an American dentist, started to transmit signals over 25 kilometres between two mountain tops. In 1876, Alexander Graham Bell invented the telephone. But the mobile phone needed different technology. It was not until nearly 100 years later, in 1973, that Dr Martin Cooper, of the American company Motorola, invented the mobile phone. Nowadays there are hundreds of millions of mobile phones in the world. Some of them can take pictures and even video.
Components	A mobile phone consists of a miniature rechargeable battery, a keypad with numbers and letters, a radio receiver and a radio transmitter and an LCD for numbers and letters.
Operation	The rechargeable battery provides power for the mobile phone. When you dial a number, your phone transmits a signal to the nearest base station. There are thousands of base stations in each country. The base station transmits a signal to another base station and, eventually, sends a signal to the phone that you are calling. When the person answers, his or her phone transmits a signal to your phone, so now there is two-way communication with two different signals.
The future	Mobile phones will probably become complete personal computers, with word processing, spreadsheets and database programs.

Lesson 1: Vocabulary

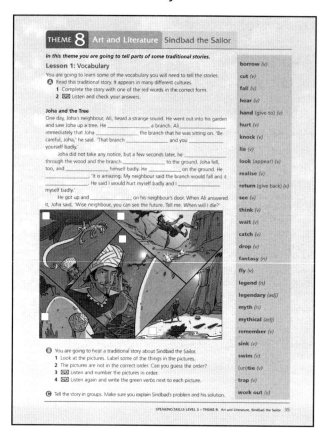

Phonology

Making yourself clear – minimal pairs with vowel, consonant and stress changes

Linking – C + V: carrying sound of final consonant on to beginning of the next word

Linking – V + V: with intrusive /j/, /r/ and /w/

Linking – suppressed consonants: e.g., *I go(t) the job*

Shifting word stress: e.g., *'hibernate – hiber'nation*

Introduction

Write the phrase *Traditional stories* on the board. Ask students to name any characters from traditional stories in their culture. Ask what kind of character the person is. Write on the board and check / teach the words as you go – *a hero, a heroine, a fool, a trickster, a wise man or woman.* Point out that these are the main characters in traditional stories.

If students did Level 2, remind them of Joha (they might have their own name in their culture for this character) and remind them also that he is a wise fool – he does foolish things for sensible reasons. Sometimes he tricks other people and sometimes he is tricked. If they didn't do Level 2, write the name on the board, say the name and see if any students recognise it.

Whether the students know the character of Joha or not, if you have the cassette or CD, play or tell the story of Joha and the donkey (from Speaking Level 2 Theme 8, Lesson 4). Pause before the end and get students to predict the ending.

Put students into pairs to try to remember the basic story.

In the course to date, students have studied the following areas of spoken English and phonology. Take every opportunity to practise these points further in this theme. In particular, whenever students are reading text or doing pairwork, monitor and note failure to link sounds in an English way.

Speaking skills

Stating sources – *According to ...*

Talking about importance and relevance – *It's not important how good his work is.*

Indicating partial comprehension – *I don't understand the part about ...*

Using the definite article with proper nouns – *The Himalayas* but *Mount Everest*

Comparing more than two things – *the biggest lake in the world*

Using, making and pronouncing question tags – *A grave is a hole in the ground, isn't it?*

Describing a device – *definition, history, components, operation, the future*

Exercise A

1 Set for individual work then pairwork checking. Do not feed back.

2 Play the recording. Feed back by getting students to tell the story round the class.

Answer

Target words in italics

One day, Joha's neighbour, Ali, heard a strange sound. He went out into his garden and saw Joha up a tree. He *was cutting* a branch. Ali *realised* immediately that Joha *was cutting* the branch that he was sitting on. 'Be careful, Joha,' he said. 'That branch *will fall* and you*'ll / will hurt* yourself badly.'

Joha did not take any notice, but a few seconds later, he *cut* through the wood and the branch *fell* to the ground. Joha fell, too, and *hurt* himself badly. He *lay* on the ground. He *thought*, 'It is amazing. My neighbour said the branch would fall and it *fell*. He said I would hurt myself badly and I *hurt* myself badly.'

He got up and *knocked* on his neighbour's door. When Ali answered it, Joha said 'Wise neighbour, you can see the future. Tell me. When will I die?'

Exercise B

Refer students to the pictures. Explain that they show scenes from a story about Sindbad the Sailor. Elicit any information that students have about Sindbad – especially the fact that he is legendary – in other words, he may have been a real person, but the stories of his adventures have been exaggerated. Explain that some people believe he came from Basra (Iraq), while others think he was born in Sohar in Oman. Students who did Level 2 Listening Theme 8 should be able to say quite a lot about this.

1   Give students plenty of time to look at the pictures and try to label things. Feed back, ideally onto an OHT of the pictures. Make sure students have labelled at least the following: *cliff, turban, beach, egg, bird, snake, diamonds.*

2   Set for pairwork. Do not confirm or correct.

3   Play the recording. Students number the pictures, then discuss in pairs or groups.

4   Refer students to the green verbs. Emphasise that they only have to write the verbs, not the nouns or

adjectives. Play the recording again, pausing after a target word – see marked-up tapescript on page 158 of this book. Feed back, ideally adding the verbs to the OHT of the pictures.

Answers

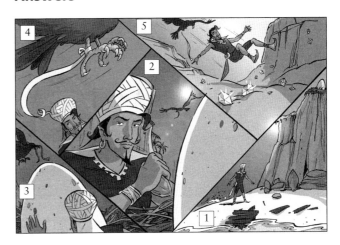

Methodology notes

1   There is a preview in this story of the use of the past perfect for events before the time of the story, e.g., *His ship had sunk* … Do not highlight this unless a student notices it.

2   It is not easy to write the verbs under the pictures because they are in the infinitive in the list and in the past or past participle form in the story. However, it is important that students should be able to immediately associate, e.g., *caught* with *catch*, so they can recover the meaning in real time.

Exercise C

Point out that there is a problem and a solution in the story of Sindbad and the roc. This is very common in traditional stories with heroes who go on a journey. They face many problems and come up with fantastic solutions.

Elicit the problem – Sindbad is trapped on an island with no food – and the solution – he gets the bird to carry him to another island.

Set for pairwork. Monitor and assist. Do not expect very high standards of storytelling at this point, but pick students up on any confusion of who did what – not too difficult here if the students remember to use *it* as the pronoun for the bird.

Point out that when we are telling stories, we must not bore the listener – so we should try to refer to the same thing in different ways – e.g., *the roc, the bird, the creature* – or simply *Sinbad* and *he*. Point out also, however, that we must not confuse the listener, so we must use the characters' names occasionally, otherwise we get sentences like *He gave it to him*, and we don't know who is who.

Elicit examples of lexical cohesion in the story of *Joha and the tree*, e.g.,

Ali; neighbour; he; his (garden); my neighbour Joha; he; his (neighbour's door) tree; branch; wood; it

Closure

Write the word *fantastic* on the board. Elicit the normal meaning = *very nice / good*. Point out that it also means impossible, from the word *fantasy* = not real. Establish that solutions in traditional stories are often fantastic – they couldn't happen in real life. Ask *What is fantastic about Sindbad's solution in the story of the roc?* Elicit reasons. It is probably best to do this as a whole-group activity.

Answers

Possible reasons are:

In real life, the bird would feel him on its leg and it would attack him. Even if it didn't feel him, it wouldn't be able to fly with a man tied to its leg.

In real life, the turban / cloth would not be strong enough to hold him. He would probably fall off when the bird was high in the sky and kill himself.

Language and culture note

Some English speakers say *fantastical* to express this meaning of impossible.

Lesson 2: Speaking

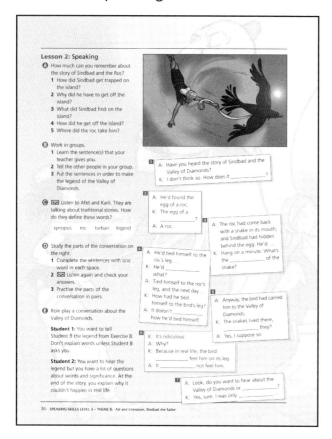

Introduction

Write these three green words on the board:

fantasy   legend   myth

Check / teach the key differences in meaning, viz:

fantasy = story that is not true and everyone knows it; often contains strange creatures and fantastic events

legend = story that may have truthful parts to it, but the creatures and events have been exaggerated

myth = story or fact that is not true, but that some people believe, or believed at one time

Point out that the meanings of the last two are so close that books of traditional stories are often called, e.g., *The Myths and Legends of Greece.*

Ask students to talk about the most famous myth or legend of their culture.

Exercise A

Exploit the illustration for vocabulary.

Set the questions for pairwork. Feed back orally. Make sure students are using and pronouncing past simple forms correctly.

Answers

1 His ship sank and he swam to the shore.
2 There was no food on the island.
3 He found a roc's egg. A roc is a mythical creature.
4 He tied himself to the leg of a roc.
5 It carried him to the Valley of Diamonds.

Exercise B

Ideally, use the version of the story on page 109; photocopy it and cut it up to make a jigsaw. Mix the sentences up before you hand them out. However, on this occasion it is not vital that you do the activity this way, as the idea is for students to learn their sentence(s) before they try to put the story in order.

Alternatively, use the sentences to make a wall dictation: i.e., students stick their sentences on part of the classroom wall and can go back and look as many times as they want, but they cannot actually read the words from the piece of paper while they write.

Encourage students to move around so they are in the correct order to tell the story.

Monitor and assist.

You might like to photocopy the story in the correct order and hand it out at the end.

Answers
The correct order is as follows:

The Legend of the Valley of Diamonds

Deep in the mountains of a distant land there was a huge valley.

On the floor of the valley there were thousands of enormous diamonds.

However, it was impossible to get into the valley because the mountainsides were too steep.

But a group of clever merchants found a way to get the diamonds.

The men threw pieces of meat into the valley.

The meat hit the diamonds and some of them stuck in the flesh.

Huge birds called rocs visited the valley regularly to catch snakes.

When the rocs found pieces of meat in the valley, they picked them up.

The rocs carried the meat and the diamonds up into the sky.

Some of the diamonds fell out of the meat and the merchants caught them.

Exercise C

Write the four words from the yellow box on the board. Point out that students know the meanings of most of these words already, but the task is to listen for how the people on the recording define each one.

Set for pairwork. Play the recording. Feed back orally.

Answers

synopsis	a summary of a story
roc	a mythical bird
turban	a piece of cloth that you wear around your head
legend	a story in which fantastic things happen

Exercise D

1   Give students plenty of time to look at the extracts from the conversation and think of / remember the missing words. Note that there is a lot of revision work in the conversation, including talking about significance, indicating partial understanding and using question tags.

2   Play the recording again, pausing after each extract (marked on the tapescript on page 158 of this book with //).

3   Set for pairwork. Monitor and assist. Drill some of the target sentences. Get some of the better students to perform extracts in front of the class.

Answers
Target words in italics

1   A: Have you heard the story of Sindbad and the Valley of Diamonds?
     K: I don't think so. How does it *go*?

2   A: He'd found the egg of a roc.
     K: The egg of a *what*?
     A: A roc.

3   A: The roc had come back with a snake in its mouth, and Sindbad had hidden behind the egg. He'd …
     K: Hang on a minute. What's the *significance* of the snake?

4   A: He'd tied himself to the roc's leg …
     K: He'd *done* what?
     A: Tied himself to the roc's leg and the next day …
     K: How had he tied himself to the bird's leg?
     A: It doesn't *matter* how he'd tied himself.

5   A: Anyway, the bird had carried him to the Valley of Diamonds.
     K: The snakes lived there, *didn't* they?
     A: Yes, I suppose so.

6 K: It's ridiculous.

   A: Why?

   K: Because in real life, the bird *would* feel him on its leg.

   A: It *might* not feel him.

7 K: Look, do you want to hear about the Valley of Diamonds or *not*?

   A: Yes, sure. I was only *saying* ...

Methodology note

There are several examples of the past perfect again in this conversation, including one case where the past participle is the target word. Once again this is to preview the focus on this point about storytelling in Lesson 3.

Exercise E

Set up the role play carefully. Make sure students realise it is an opportunity to practise storytelling (Student A) and to use some of the language from previous themes (Student B). You might like to swap round after some time so both students get a chance to take each role.

Closure

Get one or two of the better pairs to role-play their conversation in front of the class.

The Legend of the Valley of Diamonds

Deep in the mountains of a distant land there was a huge valley.

On the floor of the valley there were thousands of enormous diamonds.

However, it was impossible to get into the valley because the mountainsides were too steep.

But a group of clever merchants found a way to get the diamonds.

The men threw pieces of meat into the valley.

The meat hit the diamonds and some of them stuck in the flesh.

Huge birds called rocs visited the valley regularly to catch snakes.

When the rocs found pieces of meat in the valley, they picked them up.

The rocs carried the meat and the diamonds up into the sky.

Some of the diamonds fell out of the meat and the merchants caught them.

Lesson 3: Learning new skills

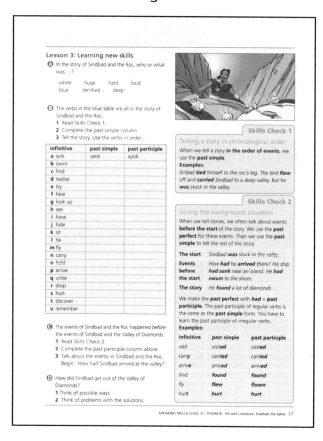

Introduction

Exploit the visual. Get students to tell the story of the legend of the Valley of Diamonds again.

Exercise A

Set for pairwork. Feed back by building up the table on the board. Then elicit sentences containing the adjective and noun in each case. Try to get students to do a little better than, e.g., *The egg was white* in each case. For example, *Sindbad saw a large white egg in the sand. Suddenly, a huge roc flew down.* Point out that in stories we often add an adjective before a noun, especially an extreme adjective like *huge* or *terrified*.

Answers

white	the egg
huge	the roc
hard	the shell (of the egg)
loud	the noise (of the roc)
blue	the sky
terrified	Sindbad
deep	the valley

Exercise B

1 and 2 Follow the instructions as written. Feed back, building up the first part of the table on the board.

3 Remind students that they told the story in Lesson 1. Now, however, they have learnt or at least checked some of the vocabulary and the grammar. Set for pairwork. Monitor and assist. Feed back by getting students to tell the whole story round the class.

Answers

2 See after Exercise C.

3 Model answer

sink	Sindbad's ship sank.
swim	He swam to the shore of a desert island.
find	He found a large white ball.
realise	He realised that it was a roc's egg.
try	He tried to open the egg.
heard	He heard a loud noise.
look up	He looked up into the blue sky.
see	He saw a huge bird coming down towards him.
have	The roc had a snake in its mouth.
hide	Sindbad hid near the egg.
sit	The bird sat on the egg.
tie	Sindbad tied himself to its leg.
fly	The bird flew off in the morning to find food.
carry	It carried Sindbad high into the sky.

hold	Sindbad held on tight to the bird.
arrive	They arrived at a deep valley.
untie	Sindbad untied himself from the bird's leg.
drop	He dropped to the ground.
hurt	He hurt himself when he landed.
discover	He discovered a lot of diamonds all around him.
remember	Sindbad remembered the legend of the Valley of Diamonds …

Methodology note

Students have already had a go at telling the story in Lesson 1. By now, however, they should be much better – more accurate and more fluent.

Language and culture note

There is a style of storytelling in Arabic in which you can begin in the equivalent of past simple, but once you have established the tense, you can switch to the equivalent of present simple. It is necessary for Arab students to learn consciously, therefore, that they must keep using the past simple when they tell a story. Of course, we can tell a whole story in the present simple in English, but, once again, we cannot change the tense during the telling. If we start: *Sindbad's ship sinks and he swims to the shore*, we must keep using the present simple.

Exercise C

1 Refer students to Skills Check 2. While they are reading, draw a time line on the board. Add the information as shown in the order given by the numbers.

His ship **had sunk**.	He **had swum** to the shore …	Sindbad **was** stuck in a deep valley	He **found** a lot of diamonds on the ground
2	3	1	4

Point out that some events *had happened* before the start of the story.

Highlight the key points about forming past participles, as demonstrated by the chosen examples in the Skills Check, viz:

infinitive	past simple	past participle	notes
visit	*visited*	*visited*	*regular verbs ending in a consonant = add ed for both past simple and past participle*
carry	*carried*	*carried*	*regular verbs ending in C+y = change y to ied for both past simple and past participle*
arrive	*arrived*	*arrived*	*regular verbs ending in e = add d for both past simple and past participle*
find	*found*	*found*	*some irregular verbs have the same form for past simple and past participle*
fly	*flew*	*flown*	*some irregular verbs have different forms for past simple and past participle*
hurt	*hurt*	*hurt*	*many irregular verbs ending in t have the same form for all three parts*

2   Set for individual work then pairwork checking. Feed back by building up the rest of the table on the board. Drill the groups of words.

3   This is really just an extended drill. Students need to put the action verbs into the past perfect. Point out the pronunciation of *had* – it is completely elided with pronouns, e.g., *he'd*, and pronounced with schwa in other situations.

Answers

2   (also Exercise B 2)

	infinitive	past simple	past participle
a	sink	*sank*	*sunk*
b	swim	swam	swum
c	find	found	found
d	realise	realised	realised
e	try	tried	tried
f	hear	heard /hɜːd/	heard /hɜːd/
g	look up	looked up	looked up
h	see	saw	seen
i	have	had	had
j	hide	hid	hidden
k	sit	sat	sat
l	tie	tied	tied
m	fly	flew	flown
n	carry	carried	carried
o	hold	held	held
p	arrive	arrived	arrived
q	untie	untied	untied
r	drop	dropped	dropped
s	hurt	hurt	hurt
t	discover	discovered	discovered
u	remember	remembered	remembered

3   Model answer

sink	Sindbad's ship had sunk.
swim	He had swum to the shore of a desert island.
find	He had found a large white ball.
realise	He had realised that it was a roc's egg.
try	He had tried to open the egg.
heard	He had heard a loud noise.
look up	He had looked up into the blue sky.
see	He had seen a huge bird coming down towards him.
have	The roc had had a snake in its mouth.
hide	Sindbad had hidden near the egg.
sit	The bird had sat on the egg.
tie	Sindbad had tied himself to its leg.
fly	The bird had flown off in the morning to find food.
carry	It had carried Sindbad to a deep valley.
hold	Sindbad had held on tight to the bird.
arrive	They had arrived at another island.
untie	Sindbad had untied himself from the bird's leg.
drop	He had dropped to the ground.
hurt	He had hurt himself when he landed.
discover	He had discovered a lot of diamonds all around him.
remember	Sindbad had remembered the legend of the Valley of Diamonds …

Methodology note

Point out, if you like, that it is very rare to give a lot of background events with the past perfect. If a storyteller really wants to *flash back* – teach the word if you wish – to a complete earlier event, he or she will start in the past perfect, then move to the simple past when the fact of the events having happened earlier is established in the listener's mind.

Language and culture note

The way we establish the time reference in past perfect, then switch to the past simple, is very similar to the way Arabic starts in the past simple and switches to the present simple – but we don't do it with these tenses in English.

Exercise D

Remind students that traditional stories often have problems for the hero or heroine to solve.

1   Set for pairwork. Feed back orally. Accept any reasonable (or fantastic!) solution. The students do have to get the correct ending – see Lesson 4.
2   Elicit problems with the solutions. Encourage students to use the phrase *In real life* … to begin their objections.

Methodology note

Don't spend too long on this exercise. There is a more extended version at the beginning of the next lesson.

Closure

Test students on past simple and past participle forms, e.g., say an infinitive and get the other two forms OR say one of the other forms and get the infinitive.

Put students into pairs to test each other.

Lesson 4: Applying new skills

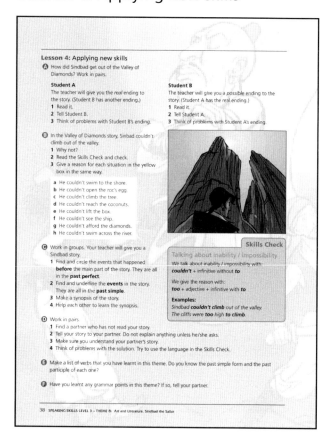

Introduction

Further test students on the three forms of the verbs from Lesson 3.

Exercise A

Put students into pairs. Refer each to the correct page of the Course Book. Student A's ending is on page 62, Student B's ending is on page 63.

Answers

Possible objections to each ending:

Student A's ending (the real one)

In real life, the bird would not think Sindbad was a piece of meat. Even if it thought he was meat, it would hurt him in picking him up and it wouldn't be able to take off with a man attached to the meat.

Student B's ending:

In real life, the men at the top of the cliffs couldn't hear him. Even if they could hear him, their ropes would be too short to reach him.

Exercise B

Exploit the visual.

Set for pairwork. Feed back onto the board. Make sure students are pronouncing *couldn't* correctly and the sounds in *too* and *to* (i.e., /uː/ for *too*, schwa for *to*).

Answers

a   He couldn't swim to the shore.
     The shore was too far (away) to swim to.

b   He couldn't open the roc's egg.
     The shell was too hard to break.

c   He couldn't climb the tree.
     The tree was too tall to climb.

d   He couldn't reach the coconuts.
     The coconuts were too high to reach.

e   He couldn't lift the box.
     The box was too heavy to lift.

f   He couldn't see the ship.
     The ship was too far away to see.

g   He couldn't afford the diamonds.
     The diamonds were too expensive to buy.

h   He couldn't swim across the river.
     The river was too wide to swim across.

Exercise C

Put students into groups. Refer each group to the correct page of the Course Book or give out a photocopy of the picture and story (pages 116 and 117 of this book). Group A's story is on page 65 of the Course Book, Group B's story is on page 67.

Teacher-pace the work through the four stages of the activity.

Exercise D

1   Let students find their own partner for pairwork.
    They need to check that their partner has not read
    their story by asking *Have you heard the story of
    Sindbad and the ...?*

2 and 3 Monitor and assist. Check that students are
    asking about new words or strange ideas.

4   Remind students about the fantastic nature of most
    solutions. Get them to think of problems with the
    solutions in the stories they have heard. Feed back.

Answers

Possible problems with Group A's solution

Sindbad and the River

In real life, Sindbad would fall off the raft as soon as
he fell asleep. Even if he stayed on the raft, there would
be parts of the tunnel that were too small for the raft
to pass through.

Possible problems with Group B's solution

Sindbad and the Coconuts

In real life, the men wouldn't be able to throw the
stones high enough to hit the monkeys. The monkeys
would run off, rather than throw the coconuts at the
men.

Exercise E

Set for individual work then pairwork discussion.

Exercise F

Set for individual work then pairwork discussion.

Closure

Elicit verbs and grammar points that people come up
with in Exercises E and F.

PHOTOCOPIABLE

Group A

Sindbad and the Strange River

Sindbad was trapped on a desert island. His ship had sunk and he couldn't get off. He had found a lot of diamonds on the beach. He had saved a small amount of food from the sinking ship, but he couldn't find anything else to eat. He had made a shelter from pieces of the ship that had washed ashore. The cliffs were too steep to climb, but he had found a place where a fast-flowing river disappeared into a tunnel in the sand. How did Sindbad get off the island?

He made a raft from his shelter and filled his pockets with diamonds. He tied himself and his food to the raft. He pushed it into the river. After several days, he fell asleep, and when he woke up he had arrived in a beautiful land.

PHOTOCOPIABLE

Group B

Sindbad and the Coconuts

Sindbad was in a strange country. He was very hungry and he couldn't find anything to eat. He had met some people who had offered to show him a place with lots of coconuts. He had gone with the men, and after some time they had arrived at a stony beach with lots of coconut palms. Sindbad had seen that the trees were too tall and too smooth to climb. Just then, he heard a lot of noise, and when he looked up, he saw that there were hundreds of monkeys in the tops of the palm trees.

How did the men get the coconuts?

They picked up the stones and threw them up at the monkeys. The monkeys got angry, picked the coconuts and threw them at the men.

Lesson 1: Vocabulary

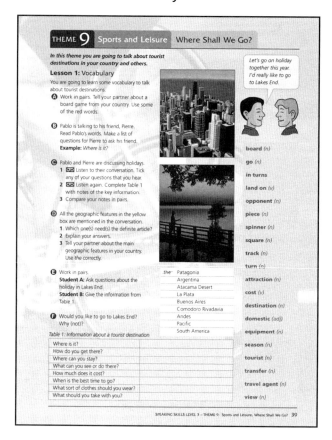

In this theme, there is revision of three skills points from the course to date:

- using the definite article with proper nouns;
- comparing more than two things;
- indicating partial comprehension.

Introduction

If students did Level 2, remind them about this theme at that level – talking about the rules of a board game. If not, point out that sports and leisure includes physical games like football and tennis, and mental games like chess and backgammon. Ideally, take in a draughts set and elicit how to play the game, using as many of the red words as possible in the process. If you have a multicultural group, put students into culture groups and ask them to think of a board game from their culture. Note that the game does not have to use a physical board – a game played with stones on the sand is OK, because it will involve the same language.

Ideally it should be a traditional game, so that it is less likely that people from other cultures will know the game (hence there will be a true information gap in Exercise A). If all your students are from the same culture, put students into pairs to think of a game and work out the rules in English. Then go straight to the feedback stage of Exercise A below.

Exercise A

Put students into pairs. If you have a multicultural group, make sure that each pair has people from different cultures. Monitor. Feed back, getting some of the most lucid people to explain the rules of their games. Ask questions to check the rules.

Methodology note

On this occasion, the majority of the green words only appear in the taped conversation – they are not actually written on the page.

Exercise B

Take in travel advertisements from newspapers and the web. Put students into groups of four or five and hand an advertisement to each group of students. Depending on their reading skills, they should be able to find at least some of the information in each advert about where, when, how much, type of accommodation, what is included in the price, etc. Ask students to give the details of their place to the rest of the class. Get the students to choose one of the places to go to.

Refer students to the cartoon and the speech bubble. Elicit a few questions and write them on the board. Set for pairwork. Feed back, building up a list of questions on the board. Ideally, all the questions from Table 1 (at the bottom of the page) should be elicited, but do not worry if some are missed. The students will hear them in the conversation.

Exercise C

1   Set for individual work and pairwork checking. Play the recording. Feed back, making sure the form of the question is correct in each case. Refer students to Table 1 and highlight any additional questions that the students have missed.
2   Make sure students understand that they only have to write notes – they could even write them in their own language. Set for individual work. Point out that many of the key words are in the yellow box. Play the recording. While students are working, make sure you have the questions from Table 1 on the board, in the same order.
3   Give plenty of time for students to compare notes. If you wish, play the recording again. Feed back, building up the table on the board. Deal with new vocabulary.

Answers

Model notes

Where is it?	Lakes End, Lake La Plata, Patagonia, Argentina, South America*
How do you get there?	plane to Buenos Aires, plane to Com Riv., 4x4 to Lake La Plata, motorboat to Lakes End.
Where can you stay?	log cabin
What can you see or do there?	views = mountains, lake do = fishing, walking, reading
How much does it cost?	$1,500 p.p. inc. transfers
When is the best time to go?	no tourist season
What sort of clothes should you wear?	clothes suitable for season; walking boots
What should you take with you?	fishing rod, books

*Students do not have to get all of this.

Exercise D

Remind students that there are rules for using the definite article with proper nouns, such as the names of places and geographic features. Give examples of *the Nile* because it is a river and *Everest* because it is a mountain.
1   Set for pairwork.
2   Feed back, building up the table on the board. Elicit reasons as you go.
3   Talk about your own country / region for a few moments. Set for pairwork. Monitor. Feed back, eliciting some of the more interesting descriptions.
Drill the words in the yellow box. Point out that the stress is in the expected place on all these proper nouns – i.e., the first syllable of two-syllable words and the one before the last in multi-syllable words (with the exception of *A'merica*).

Answers

~~the~~	Pata'gonia	Because it's a region.
~~the~~	Argen'tina	Because it's a country.
the	Ata'cama	Because it's a desert.
~~the~~	La 'Plata	Because it's a lake.
~~the~~	'Buenos 'Aires	Because it's a city.
~~the~~	Como'doro Riva'davia	Because it's a town.
the	'Andes	Because they are mountains.
the	Pa'cific	Because it's an ocean.
~~the~~	South A'merica	Because it's a continent.

Exercise E

Drill the questions.

Set up the role play. Remind students about asking about new words, i.e.,

    meaning
    pronunciation
    spelling

Remind them also about indicating partial comprehension, i.e.,

> *I don't understand the part about ...*
> *Can you explain the bit about ...?*

Monitor and assist.

Feed back, getting different pairs to do different parts of the conversation.

Exercise F

Do as general class discussion. Elicit some useful language for talking about pros and cons of holiday destinations, e.g.,

> *interesting*
> *getting away from it all*
> *boring / nothing to do*
> *exciting*
> *tiring*
> *scary*
> *remote*

Closure

Refer students to the green words and check pronunciation and meaning. Note that although most of these words don't appear on the page, they have all appeared in the conversation.

Highlight stress and the fact that the multi-syllable words again obey the common rules of stress as follows:

first syllable of two	one before the last
'agent	*a'ttraction*
'season	*desti'nation*
'tourist	*do'mestic*
'transfer	*e'quipment*
'travel	

Lesson 2: Speaking

skiing	on a mountain, at a ski resort
hiking	anywhere, but most interestingly in hills or valleys and through forests
fly fishing	in a river
scuba diving	in the sea, usually near the coast
snorkelling	in shallow water near the coast
sightseeing	anywhere, but most interestingly where there are beautiful views, ruins or old works of architecture
paragliding	usually on the coast, but also from hills or mountains
sunbathing	anywhere where there is sun, but usually on holiday on a beach
cycling	anywhere, but most interestingly on country roads or tracks
mountain climbing	on a mountain!
horse riding	anywhere, but most interestingly in hills or valleys and through forests

Introduction

Check pronunciation of the green words again.

Check the meaning with questions:

When is the tourist season in your country?

Are there domestic flights in your country? What are the destinations?

How much does it cost to fly to … [suitable destination]?

What are the main tourist attractions in your country?

What equipment do you need for skiing? What about fishing?

Have you ever used an online travel agent? Why (not)?

Refer students to the pictures and ask them where they can do each activity – a *generic* location not a specific one, i.e.,

Exercise A

1   Set for pairwork. Feed back, writing the words on the board. Check pronunciation, especially stress. Note that several break the pattern this time. Point out the difference between *walking* and *hiking* – the second word is a leisure activity, rather than just a method of travel.

2   Set for pairwork. Feed back with general discussion. Get other students to ask about new proper nouns – pronunciation and spelling, if the students are not from the same country.

3   General discussion. Push students to give reasons and teach any useful vocabulary. Highlight the *-ing* (i.e., gerund) form after *like* and *hate* when these verbs are used to talk about experience.

4   General discussion, as before. Highlight the infinitive form *to do* after *like* and *hate* when they are used to talk about preferences / wishes. This will become even more relevant in Lesson 3.

Answers (stress)

1   'skiing
2   'hiking
3   'fishing
4   ('scuba) 'diving
5   'snorkelling
6   'sightseeing
7   'paragliding
8   'sunbathing
9   'cycling
10 'mountain climbing (phrase is stressed),
    mountai'neering
11 'horse riding (phrase is stressed)

Language and culture note

Scuba sounds like a word English has borrowed from another language – Hawaiian perhaps, or Finnish? As aficionados will know, it is an acronym for *self contained underwater breathing apparatus* – in other words, a gas bottle on your back. *Snorkelling* comes from German, incidentally.

Exercise B

Work through the example. Deal with the new vocabulary in the answers. Set for pairwork. Feed back orally. Practise the questions and answers – you ask each question and invite a student to give you the appropriate answer.

Highlight the use of *take* + a method of transport. Show that it can be extended:

fly   take a flight
sail take a boat / ferry
drive take a 4x4; taxi; bus; coach

Answers

1   Where is it?
    It's two hundred miles north of the Arctic Circle in Sweden.

2   What should you take with you?
    Take a fishing rod and a good pair of walking boots.

3   How much does it cost?
    The price is $675 per person for two nights, based on two people sharing.

4   When is the best time to go?
    You can go from May to September, but remember that temperatures are very high in late July and August.

5   What can you see or do there?
    You can see nature in its original form, before Man arrived to spoil things.

6   How do you get there?
    You fly to Rome and then you take a domestic flight or a train to Naples.

7   Where can you stay?
    You live on the boat, which has seven cabins.

8   What sort of clothes should you wear?
    You need two sets – one for cycling and one for hiking.

Exercise C

You can refer students to the relevant pages at the back of the Course Book as follows:

Text A: page 62
Text B: page 63
Text C: page 64
Text D: page 66

Alternatively, you can photocopy the texts (on pages 125–128 of this book) before the lesson and hand them out at this point.

Follow the procedure as before with this type of activity, i.e.,

• Put students into groups, A, B, C and D, and give copies of one of the texts to each group. Give them time to read the text, help each other to understand it and agree on a set of notes.

• Put students into new groups, preferably of four, each of which must have at least one A, one B, one C and one D student. Students can refer to their notes, but they cannot look back at the original text.

Monitor and assist, especially with new vocabulary at the first stage, but as far as possible let the students help each other to understand the text.

Note whether any chairperson appears in any of the groups at any of the stages. If one does, refer to this at the end of the activity, i.e., point out that in Group X one person organised the activity. Say you will come back to this in Lesson 4.

Closure

Ask students which holiday they would like to go on. Elicit ideas and reasons.

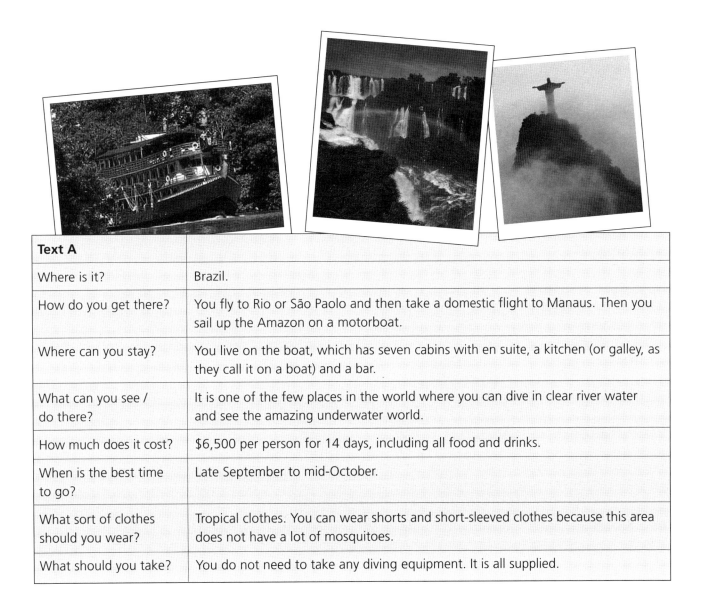

Text A	
Where is it?	Brazil.
How do you get there?	You fly to Rio or São Paolo and then take a domestic flight to Manaus. Then you sail up the Amazon on a motorboat.
Where can you stay?	You live on the boat, which has seven cabins with en suite, a kitchen (or galley, as they call it on a boat) and a bar.
What can you see / do there?	It is one of the few places in the world where you can dive in clear river water and see the amazing underwater world.
How much does it cost?	$6,500 per person for 14 days, including all food and drinks.
When is the best time to go?	Late September to mid-October.
What sort of clothes should you wear?	Tropical clothes. You can wear shorts and short-sleeved clothes because this area does not have a lot of mosquitoes.
What should you take?	You do not need to take any diving equipment. It is all supplied.

Text B	
Where is it?	At the edge of space!
How do you get there?	You fly to Moscow and then travel by helicopter to a Russian air force base – the location is secret.
Where can you stay?	You stay on the military base in air force accommodation, which is basic but comfortable.
What can you see / do there?	You go up in a Mig 25, which is the fastest jet fighter in the world. You can see the curve of the Earth from this height. You then fly the plane at over 3,000 kilometres per hour.
How much does it cost?	$10,000 per person for three days, including two flights.
When is the best time to go?	Any time of the year.
What sort of clothes should you wear?	Warm clothes in winter, lightweight clothes in summer.
What should you take?	You do not need to take any equipment. It is all supplied.

Text C	
Where is it?	Two hundred kilometres north of the Arctic Circle, Sweden.
How do you get there?	You fly to Stockholm and then take a domestic flight to Kiruna. You can take a bus or a taxi to Jukkasjärvi.
Where can you stay?	You stay in the Ice Hotel, which is actually built from ice every year to a different design.
What can you see / do there?	You can go on a snowmobile safari to see reindeer and other Arctic animals.
How much does it cost?	From £675 per person based on two people sharing, including one night at the Ice Hotel and one night in the heated bungalow next door.
When is the best time to go?	You can only go in the winter, of course, from mid-December to the end of April.
What sort of clothes should you wear?	The hotel provides warm outer clothing, but you should wear warm underwear. Night-time temperatures in the hotel are around −5°C.
What should you take?	Take skis if you want to go skiing.

Text D	
Where is it?	On the western coast of Italy, near the city of Naples.
How do you get there?	You fly to Rome then take a domestic flight or a train to Naples. You then take a coach to Positano on the Mediterranean Sea.
Where can you stay?	You stay in a different hotel each night, which you get to by walking or cycling. The average walk each day is 20 kilometres, the average bike ride is 40 kilometres.
What can you see / do there?	You walk and cycle through sleepy Italian villages and some of the most beautiful countryside in the world. Every day there are wonderful views of the Mediterranean and the Apennine Mountains.
How much does it cost?	$2,395 per person for five days, including all meals, all transfers and all entrance fees to museums and gardens.
When is the best time to go?	You can go from May to September, but remember that temperatures are very high in late July and August.
What sort of clothes should you wear?	You need two sets of clothes – one for cycling and one for walking.
What should you take?	Take plenty of sun-cream, good strong walking boots and a cycling helmet.

Lesson 3: Learning new skills

Answers

Location	Where is it?
Accommodation	Where can you stay?
Attractions	What can you see or do there?
Season	When is the best time to go?
Special equipment	What should you take with you?
Suitable clothing	What sort of clothes should you wear?
Travel	How do you get there?
Cost	How much does it cost?

Exercise B

Set the three questions for individual work and pairwork checking. Play the recording. Feed back orally.

Answers

1 They are trying to agree on a holiday destination.
2 Different people want to go to different places.
3 They decide to go to the ice house.

Exercise C

Explain that, on this occasion, one group of students is going to read Skills Check 1 and the other is going to read Skills Check 2.

Follow previous procedure to get students to understand their own Skills Check in groups and then put them in pairs to complete the second part of the activity.

Play the recording for them to check their answers.

Introduction

Ask students about the unusual holidays from the previous lesson. See how much information they can remember.

Exercise A

Refer students to the illustration and elicit what is happening – the people are discussing something, probably holidays.

Refer them to the computer screen illustration. Only the word *accommodation* is completely new and this will probably be known from other learning.

Set for pairwork. Feed back orally.

Answers

Target words in italics

(**Note:** The student who should be able to supply the answer and the reason for each answer is given in brackets.)

A: I think that we *should* (B) all give an opinion and then I *suggest* (B) that we vote.

* * *

B: Well, I would like *to go* (A) to Argentina. I *think* (A) the lake sounds fantastic.

C: Do you really? I *would prefer* (A) to do something a bit more exciting. The Russian plane sounds incredible.

D: Yes, well, perhaps that's a little too exciting! *I'd rather* (A) go somewhere with beautiful views, like the lake ...

* * *

A: So, *shall* (B) we vote on it?

* * *

B: May I make a *suggestion* (B)?

A: Yes, of course.

B: I suggest *that* (B) we eliminate the lake, because it came last, and vote again.

Drill the expressions in the two Skills Checks.

Test usage by prompting with a question and eliciting an alternative choice. You can tell students the alternative in each case or let them think of one logically, e.g.,

    T: Would you like to have a cup of tea? (coffee)

S1: *I'd prefer to / I'd rather* have a cup of coffee.

Other possible prompts:

    Would you like to go to the cinema? (theatre)

    Would you like to stay for a little while longer? (go home)

    Would you like to study in the USA when you finish here? (Australia)

Important

Explain to students that they should do some research on tourist destinations in their own country for the speaking activity in the next lesson.

Closure

Make sure all the students are clear about the correct form of the second verbs, as follows. Build up the table on the board.

like	doing
would like	to do
would prefer	
would rather	do
shall	
may	
should	
let's	

Lesson 4: Applying new skills

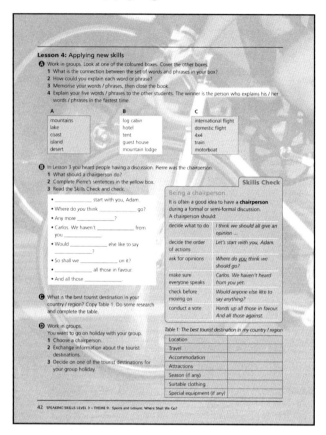

Introduction

Give the stressed syllable from each of the multi-syllable green words. Students must identify and say as follows. They can look at the green words if you wish.

/eɪ/	'agent
/træk/	a'ttraction
/neɪ/	desti'nation
/mes/	do'mestic
/kwɪp/	e'quipment
/siː/	'season
/tɔː/	'tourist
/træns/	'transfer
/træ/	'travel

Make sure students are using schwa correctly in each case.

Exercise A

Divide the class into three. Ideally, photocopy the three sets of words.

1 Give out one set to each group of students. Work with the students on the connection between the words / phrases in their set.
2 Each group has to work out how to explain the words / phrases in their set. Monitor and assist.
3 Give the groups a few more minutes to memorise the words and test each other on words and definitions.
4 Put students into groups of three. Someone must check the time it takes each student to explain their five words so the others can guess the word. If the other students have forgotten the word, they can prompt with things like: *It begins with /d/; it's got three syllables; it rhymes with pain*, etc.

Answers
1 Set A = geographic features or locations
   Set B = accommodation / places to stay
   Set C = methods of transport

Exercise B

1 Set for pairwork. Do not confirm or correct.
2 Set for individual work and pairwork checking.
3 Set for individual work and pairwork checking. Feed back orally.

Drill the sentences. Check students know what each sentence is doing – see the Skills Check. Deal with grammar points.

Answers
Target words in italics.
Let's start with you, Adam.
Where do **you** think *we should* go?*
Any more *suggestions*?
Carlos. We haven't *heard* from you, *yet*.
Would *anyone* else like to say *anything*?
So shall we *vote* on it?

Hands up all those in favour.
And all those *against*.[1]

* Note the word order: *do you think* is the question, the other part is a statement
[1] Point out that the intonation of this statement makes it sound like a question.

Exercise C

You may wish to put people into groups to do the research, but it is probably better that they work on their own when they are giving the information in Exercise D. If students have done some research, give them time to write it up in a copy of the table. Otherwise send them off to research or simply ask them to guess / make up the required information.

Methodology note

If students are all from the same country, ask for a list of tourist destinations and then for the research task, put students into groups according to which destination they like best.

Exercise D

Make sure the groups have students from different countries OR students who have chosen different destinations in the same country. Follow the instructions as written. Monitor and assist.

Closure

Feed back, getting students from each group to tell you about the destination they have chosen.

Lesson 1: Vocabulary

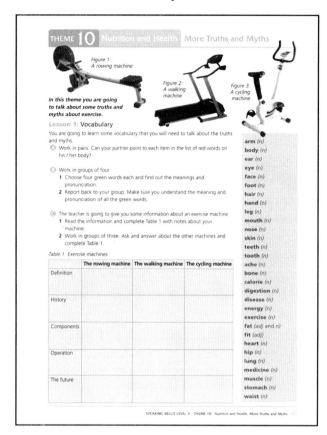

Points from Level 2 have been revised during this course.

The following points have been covered in Level 3.

Speaking tasks
Reporting on reading research
Reporting on case studies
Classifying animals
Talking about adaptations
Describing my region
Describing death customs
Describing an invention
Telling a story
Describing a tourist attraction

Phonology
Linking – C + V; V + V
Linking – suppressed plosives
Shifting word stress, e.g., 'hibernate – hiber'nation
Making and using question tags
Elided and weak form of *would*

Oral skills
Stating sources
Talking about importance and relevance
Indicating partial comprehension
Using the definite article with proper nouns
Comparing more than two things
Giving bad news
Describing a device
Talking about events before the time of the story
Presenting problems and solutions
Giving an opinion
Making a suggestion
Being a chairperson

In addition, students have learnt to give short talks on a number of topics – see Lesson 4 below.

Introduction

Check that students understand the meaning of nutrition – *what your body needs to live and grow* – and health – *the state of not being ill*. Point out that for most of this theme you are talking about the *health* side of this theme, specifically, how exercise helps with your health.

Exercise A

Set for pairwork. Feed back orally. Check the pronunciation of the red words. Do further high-speed work on the words, e.g.,

It's on your head below your nose. = *mouth*
It's all over your body. = *skin*
They're below your legs. = *feet*
They're above your hands. = *arms*

Exercise B

Refer students to the green words. Point out that they are all connected with health in some way. Ask students if they know the meaning of any of the words. Elicit some ideas, but do not confirm or correct.

Put students into groups of four.

1   See if students naturally work out how to organise the activity – in particular, see if they appoint a chairperson or if one emerges. If not, go round and simply allocate the words (i.e., first four words, you, next four words, you, etc.). Give students plenty of time for this activity. Monitor and assist, especially with working out key pronunciation points from the guidance in the dictionary.

2   Get students to start reporting back when one or two groups have finished. Monitor and assist as before.

Do high-speed checking on meaning and pronunciation, especially stress, schwas and unusual sound–sight relationships.

Exercise C

The texts are on pages 64, 65 and 67 of the Course Book. They are also reprinted on page 136 of this Teacher's Book for you to photocopy if you wish.

1   Put students into groups, A, B and C, to read one of the texts each and make notes on it. Give plenty of help with understanding the texts, as the real communicative task comes next.

2   Put students into ABC groups to complete the activity. Take away the texts or make sure that the students are not looking at them. Monitor and assist.

Closure

Drill the meaning of the green words by pointing to a part of your body (delicately!) and eliciting the appropriate word, and miming. Start slowly but speed up until you and the students are flying. Try to catch them out when they are really good. Then put the students in pairs to play the same game.

The rowing machine

A rowing machine is a kind of exercise machine. It is used for keeping fit and for exercising both the upper and lower muscles of the body.

The rowing boat was invented over 2,000 years ago. There were rowing races in Roman times. The rowing machine was invented in 1981 by two men who wanted to help professional rowers to exercise.

A rowing machine consists of a seat, a handlebar, a length of rope and a wheel. The handlebar is connected to the rope and the rope is connected to the wheel. There is an LCD in front of the wheel.

When the rower pulls on the handlebar, the rope pulls on the wheel, which turns anticlockwise. The seat moves forward. When the rower stops pulling, the seat moves back and the wheel turns clockwise. The wheel sends signals to a meter, which displays the speed on an LCD.

Rowing machines will measure the rider's heart rate and blood pressure and warn of any risk of heart attack.

The cycling machine

A cycling machine is a kind of exercise machine. It is used for keeping fit and particularly for exercising the lower muscles of the body.

The bicycle was invented in 1839 by a Scot called Kirkpatrick Macmillan.

Stationary cycles were used in the 1960s to train astronauts.

A cycling machine consists of a seat, a pair of handlebars and a pair of pedals, just like a normal bicycle. The pedals are connected to a wheel. There is an LCD on the handlebars.

When the rider pushes down on the pedals, the wheel turns. The wheel sends signals to a meter which displays the speed on an LCD.

Cycling machines will measure the rider's heart rate and blood pressure and warn of any risk of heart attack.

The walking machine

A walking machine is a kind of exercise machine. It is used for keeping fit and particularly for exercising the lower muscles of the body.

A machine called a treadmill was invented in 1875 for use on farms in America. Small animals were used to power agricultural machines. The first walking machine for humans was invented by a heart doctor, Robert Bruce, to diagnose heart and lung disease.

A walking machine consists of a pair of handles, an electric motor and a continuous band of rubber. The electric motor is controlled by the walker.

When the walker starts the motor, the band turns clockwise and the walker has to move his or her feet to remain in the same position. The walker can increase the speed of the motor so that he / she has to walk quickly or even run.

Walking machines will be fitted to desks so people with inactive jobs, like receptionists, can exercise while they are working.

Lesson 2: Speaking review (1)

Lesson 2: Speaking review (1)
Ⓐ Look at the quiz (right).
1 What is it about?
2 What do you have to do?

Ⓑ In this course you have learnt to talk about importance.
1 Complete these sentences from a conversation.
2 Listen to the first part of the conversation and check your ideas.
L: I've found this great quiz in a magazine.
A: Really. Which magazine?
L: Just a magazine.
A: But what's it called?
L: It doesn't _____
A: Well, where did you get it?
L: It's not _____

Ⓒ In this course you have learnt to talk about preferences and make suggestions.
1 Complete these sentences from the conversation with one word in each space.
2 Listen to the second part of the conversation and check your ideas.
• _____ we do it together?
• Why _____ you be the chairperson?
• _____ shall we do the quiz?
• I think we _____ do the quiz in teams.
• I'd _____ do it individually ..
• I'd _____ to work in teams ...
• We _____ heard from you yet.
• _____ take a vote on it.
• Hands up all those in _____ of teams.
• And those _____.

Ⓓ How are they going to do the quiz?
Listen to the third part, then explain.

Ⓔ In this course you have learnt to use question tags.
1 Complete these questions.
2 Listen to the fourth part of the conversation and check your ideas.
T'ai chi comes from China, _____?
Yoga is from India, _____?
Pilates was a German gymnast, _____?

SPEAKING SKILLS LEVEL 3 – THEME 10: Nutrition and Health, More Truths and Myths

So you think you know about ...

exercise?

Read each statement about exercise. Is it true or false? Decide, then turn to page 139 to find the facts!

	1	2	3	4
1 Exercise burns a lot of calories.				
2 New-style exercise types like T'ai chi, Pilates and Yoga are just silly.				
3 If a woman does a lot of exercise, she starts to look like a bodybuilder.				
4 If exercise doesn't hurt, it isn't doing you any good.				
5 If you can't exercise regularly, don't bother to exercise at all.				
6 If you jog or run with light weights on your arms or legs, you will get more benefit from the exercise.				
7 It is dangerous to start exercising when you are middle-aged.				
8 Muscle weighs more than fat, so if you exercise a lot, you actually get heavier.				
9 When you stop exercising, the muscle that you have made turns to fat.				
10 You can remove fat from a particular area of your body with the right exercise.				
11 You shouldn't exercise if you are pregnant.				
12 You shouldn't exercise if you have a cold or flu.				
13 You shouldn't exercise if you have asthma.				
14 You shouldn't swim after you have had a meal.				

Introduction

1 Say the stressed syllables from the multi-syllable green words and elicit the items – see Answers below.
2 Say the vowel sound for the single-syllable green words and elicit the items – see Answers below.
3 Play the *point and say* game and the mime game again.

Answers

1
cal	*'calorie*
gest	*di'gestion*
sease	*di'sease*
en	*'energy*
ex	*'exercise*
med	*'medicine*
mus	*'muscle*
stom	*'stomach*

2
/æ/	*fat*
/ɪ/	*fit* or *hip*
/ʌ/	*lung*
/ɑː/	*heart*
/eɪ/	*ache* or *waist*
/əʊ/	*bone*

Methodology note

You can allow students to look at the green words, as this is a sound–sight test, not a memory test.

Exercise A

Remind students of the title of the theme – *More Truths and Myths*. Remind them or explain that the noun from *true* is *truth* and things that are false are sometimes *myths* – in other words, things that people think are true but that are in fact false. Drill *truths* and *myths* – nice final consonant cluster. Remind students who did Level 2 that they learnt some truths and myths about hair, eyes, skin and teeth. This time there are more truths and myths.

Refer students to the quiz. Give students plenty of time to look, then elicit answers to the two questions.

Ask a few of the easier questions, e.g., 1, 4, 12. Elicit answers, but do not confirm or correct.

Point out that you are going to come back to the quiz later in the lesson.

Answers

1 It is about exercise.
2 Decide if the statements are true or false, i.e., truths or myths.

Exercise B

Explain that students are going to hear some friends discussing, then doing the quiz.
1   Set for individual work then pairwork checking. Elicit ideas, but do not confirm or correct.
2   Play Part 1. Give time for correction, then elicit answers. Role-play this part of the conversation with a few students.

Answers
Target words in italics.

Lucas: I've found this great quiz in a magazine.
  Ali: Really. Which magazine?
Lucas: Just a magazine.
  Ali: But what's it called?
Lucas: It doesn't *matter what it's called*.
  Ali: Well, where did you get it?
Lucas: It's not *important where I got it*.
  Ali: OK. What's it about?
Lucas: It's about exercise … you know, the truths and myths about exercise.

Language and culture note

There are two noteworthy points about the target sentences in Exercise B:
1   The fact that *matter* is a verb and therefore makes the phrase *It doesn't matter*, while *important* is an adjective and goes with *be* to make *It's not important*. Even quite advanced students sometimes mix these up and say, e.g., *It's not matter* or *It doesn't important*.
2   The speaker in each case is commenting on a question, but the repeated words are not in question word order, e.g., *what it's called* not *what is it called*. Many students fail to make this adjustment when producing reported questions.

Exercise C

Set for individual work then pairwork checking. Play Part 2. Feed back orally, insisting on full sentences. Get the sentences on the board, then drill pronunciation, intonation and rhythm.

Answers
Target words in italics
*   *Shall* we do it together?
*   Why *don't* you be the chairperson?
*   *How* shall we do the quiz?
*   I think we *should* do the quiz in teams.
*   I'd *rather* do it individually.
*   I'd *prefer* to work in teams …
*   We *haven't* heard from you yet, *Carlos*.
*   *Let's* take a vote on it.
*   Hands up all those in *favour* of teams.
*   And those *against*.

Exercise D

Set for pairwork. Play Part 3. Feed back orally. Do not confirm or correct.

Answers
Model answer
They are going to do the quiz in teams. They are going to discuss and write down each answer then tell the chairperson. The chairperson is not going to give the answers until the end.

Exercise E

1   Set for pairwork.
2   Play Part 4. Feed back, getting the correct sentences on the board.

Answers

Target words in italics

T'ai chi comes from China, *doesn't it?*

Yoga is from India, *isn't it?*

Pilates was a German gymnast, *wasn't he?*

Closure

Put students into groups of four. Follow the instructions. Point out that if they do the quiz in teams, they only need to complete columns 1 and 2. Monitor and assist the groups, but do not confirm or correct.

Deal with general vocabulary points from the quiz.

Feed back on general language points that may have arisen, but do not confirm or correct any of the quiz answers.

Lesson 3: Speaking review (2)

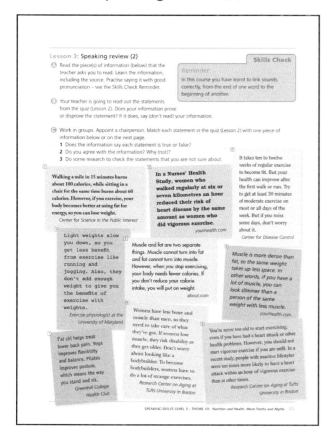

Introduction

Run through the quiz statements from Lesson 2 again and see if students agree / disagree with each one. Check vocabulary as you go.

Exercise A

Ideally, use the bigger version of the texts on pages 144–145 of this book. Cut the page into separate pieces and give one or more text(s) to each student, according to the number of students in your class. If this is not possible, get students to cover the texts that they are not supposed to be reading – although, since they are jumbled, casually glancing at another text will probably not spoil the exercise to come.

Monitor and assist with pronunciation. Refer individual students to the Skills Check Reminder as necessary. Get students to think about which statement their information proves or disproves.

Methodology note

Make the point very strongly that this information may be wrong! It is taken from a variety of Internet sources at a moment in time – further research may prove it wrong, or indeed, it may already have been proved wrong, but the revised information was not found at the time of the research. This is not an esoteric point; the 'truth' of information nowadays is rarely absolute; rather, it is a judgement about the validity of research and its results, and the credibility of the source. For example, can fat be removed from a particular area by exercise? You can find many websites that say it can, but they are the websites of exercise machine companies. Medical sites will say it is impossible. Which should you believe?

Exercise B

Read out the statements on page 44 of the Course Book. Give students plenty of time to work out whether their information is relevant to the statement. If nobody speaks up, move on to the next statement and come back to the first one when some more have been eliminated. Deal with any vocabulary issues in the texts that the students say. Get students to decide whether the information proves or disproves the statement in each case.

Exercise C

This should now be quite easy, although of course there is a lot of reading to do, albeit of texts that students have already heard. Set for pairwork. Monitor and assist.

Answers

Exercise burns a lot of calories.	1
New-style exercise types like t'ai chi, Pilates and Yoga are just silly.	7
If a woman does a lot of exercise, she starts to look like a bodybuilder.	8

If exercise doesn't hurt, it isn't doing you any good.	2
If you can't exercise regularly, don't bother to exercise at all.	3
If you jog or run with light weights on your arms or legs, you will get more benefit from the exercise.	4
It is dangerous to start exercising when you are middle-aged.	9
Muscle weighs more than fat, so if you exercise a lot, you actually get heavier.	6
When you stop exercising, the muscle that you have made turns to fat.	5
You can remove fat from a particular area of your body with the right exercise.	14
You shouldn't exercise if you are pregnant.	13
You shouldn't exercise if you have a cold or flu.	12
You shouldn't exercise if you have asthma.	10
You shouldn't swim after you have had a meal.	11

Closure

Feed back by getting a full list of the relationships between the statements and the information on the board.

1	Walking a mile in 15 minutes burns about 100 calories, while sitting in a chair for the same time burns about 60 calories. However, if you exercise, your body becomes better at using fat for energy so you can lose weight. *Center for Science in the Public Interest*
2	In a Nurses' Health Study, women who walked regularly at six or seven kilometres an hour reduced their risk of heart disease by the same amount as women who did vigorous exercise. *yourhealth.com*
3	It takes ten to twelve weeks of regular exercise to become fit. But your health can improve after the first walk or run. Try to get at least 30 minutes of moderate exercise on most or all days of the week. But if you miss some days, don't worry about it. *Center for Disease Control*
4	Light weights slow you down, so you get less benefit from exercise like running and jogging. Also, they don't add enough weight to give you the benefits of exercise with weights. *Exercise physiologist at the University of Maryland*
5	Muscle and fat are two separate things. Muscle cannot turn into fat and fat cannot turn into muscle. However, when you stop exercising, your body needs fewer calories. If you don't reduce your calorie intake, you will put on weight. *about.com*
6	Muscle is more dense than fat, so the same weight takes up less space. In other words, if you have a lot of muscle, you can look slimmer than a person of the same weight with less muscle. *yourhealth.com*
7	T'ai chi helps treats lower back pain. Yoga improves flexibility and balance. Pilates improves posture, which means the way you stand and sit. *Greenhill College Health Club*
8	Women have less bone and muscle than men, so they need to take care of what they've got. If women lose muscle, they risk disability as they get older. Don't worry about looking like a bodybuilder. To become bodybuilders, women have to do a lot of strange exercises. *Research Center on Aging at Tufts University in Boston*
9	You're never too old to start exercising, even if you have had a heart attack or other health problems. However, you should not start vigorous exercise if you are unfit. In a recent study, people with inactive lifestyles were ten times more likely to have a heart attack within an hour of vigorous exercise than at other times. *Research Center on Aging at Tufts University in Boston*

10 A 1994 study of Swedish cross-country skiers found that heavy exercise at low temperatures that involved breathing large volumes of cold air brought on asthma attacks.
wellness.ucdavis.edu

However, if asthmatics take their medicine before exercise, they should have no problems. Swimming, particularly, is a very good form of exercise for people suffering from asthma. Many Olympic athletes, including several gold medal winners, have had asthma.
healthsquare.com

11 After a meal, blood is diverted to the stomach and intestines to help digest food. If you try to exercise, your leg and arm muscles compete for blood with your digestive system. In most cases, both systems suffer. You don't move easily and you often develop stomachache or cramp – tightness in leg muscles. However, this is only true if you have had a heavy meal like beefburger and chips. You can go swimming after light meals, such as pasta and salad, without any problems at all.
ivillage.com

12 If you have cold symptoms above the neck and you don't have a fever, it is probably safe to do light exercise. Indeed, research has shown that light exercise helps your body to work more efficiently, so it may actually help you to fight the symptoms better. However, if there are symptoms of flu, such as fever, extreme tiredness or aching muscle, do not exercise. In addition, you should not exercise if you have any lung infection.
about.com

13 Pregnant women should try to exercise moderately for at least 30 minutes on most, if not all, days, unless they have received medical advice to rest. Swimming, stationary cycling, walking and aerobics are especially good. Pregnant women get all the normal benefits of exercise – feeling better physically and emotionally, stronger muscles and bones – but they also get added benefits. In particular, exercise can prevent a kind of diabetes that can develop during pregnancy. However, check with your doctor before starting any exercise programme.
pregnancy-info.net

14 You cannot lose fat from one part of your body if you are still overweight in general. The genes that you get from your parents decide where you lose fat from first. For most people, fat is lost from the waist before the hips.
Exercise physiologist at the University of Maryland

Lesson 4: Speaking review (4)

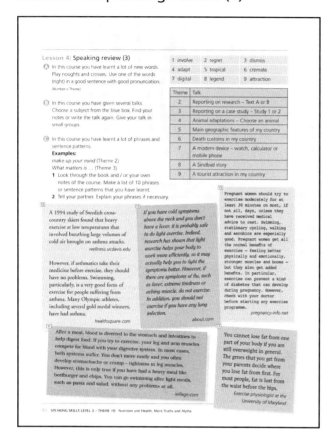

Introduction

Remind students that you have talked about many different topics or themes during this course. Ask students to tell you some things they have learnt during the course – facts / information first, then words, then structures / sentence patterns. Allow them to flick back through the book, looking at themes, word lists and Skills Checks while you are talking.

Exercise A

If you haven't played this game before (called *Tic-Tac-Toe* in North America), show the students how to play. Set for group work, or play one game first to show how it is done. Monitor and make sure that sentences are well-formed, with good pronunciation. If students are stuck, they can look back at the relevant theme.

Exercise B

Follow the procedure as written. Remember that many of the texts are at the back of the Student Book.

Exercise C

1 Set for individual work. Monitor and assist. Check pronunciation, then drill.
2 Set for pairwork checking. Monitor and assist.

Answers

Some of the useful phrases / sentence patterns from this course are as follows:

phrases
to sound good
to make up one's mind
to change one's mind
according to …
to be (un)happy with a decision
too many choices
ignore a problem
deal with / handle conflict
hope a problem will go away
accept a job
a good / bad influence
Nowadays, …
work out the solution
In real life, (X would happen)
tourist season
domestic flight
travel agent

sentence patterns
The more (choice I have), the harder (it is to make a decision).
It doesn't matter if / who / where, etc.
It's not important if / who / where, etc.
What matters is …
What's important / relevant is …
I don't understand the part about …
What's the significance of …?
Can anyone explain the bit about …?

These must / could / might be …
She's passed away.
You're fired.
A / An … is used for …ing …
Sindbad couldn't climb out of the valley.
The cliffs were too high to climb.
I'd prefer to do …
I'd rather do …
May I make a suggestion?
We should all give an opinion.
That's true.
I'm afraid I've got some really bad news.

Closure

Feed back on Exercise C, getting a list of the most common phrases and sentence patterns on the board and checking meaning and usage.

Word Lists: Thematic

THEME 1
Education, It's Not My Style

aural *(adj)*

kinaesthetic *(adj)*

learner *(n)*

mode *(n)*

visual *(adj)*

discussion *(n)*

involve *(v)*

point *(n)*

project *(n)*

research *(n)*

role play *(n)*

suppose *(v)*

THEME 2
Daily Life, Are You a Maximizer or a Satisficer?

angry *(adj)*

apologise *(v)*

argue *(v)*

argument *(n)*

calm *(adj)*

deal with *(v)*

matter *(n* and *v)*

sorry *(adj)*

upset *(adj)*

wrong *(adj)*

alternative *(n)*

behave *(v)*

change (mind) *(v)*

choose *(v)*

decide *(v)*

decision *(n)*

make up (mind) *(v)*

regret *(n* and *v)*

THEME 3
Work and Business, The Person and the Problem

colleague *(n)*

concentrate *(v)*

concentration *(n)*

distract *(v)*

organise *(v)*

TO DO list *(n)*

urgent *(adj)*

cause *(n)*

conflict *(n)*

dismiss *(v)*

handle *(v)*

ignore *(v)*

management *(n)*

manager *(n)*

organisation *(n)*

worker *(n)*

THEME 4
Science and Nature, Adapting to the Climate

animal *(n)*

carbon *(n)*

convert *(v)*

cycle *(n)*

gas *(n)*

hydrogen *(n)*

liquid *(n)*

nitrogen *(n)*

oxygen *(n)*

plant *(n)*

process *(n)*

solid *(n)*

adapt *(v)*

amphibian *(n)*

backbone *(n)*

cold-blooded *(adj)*

feather *(n)*

fur *(n)*

insect *(n)*

mammal *(n)*

reptile *(n)*

scale *(n)*

skin *(n)*

warm-blooded *(adj)*

THEME 5
The Physical World, Do You Know Your Region?

area (n)

climate (n)

location (n)

population (n)

region (n)

temperature (n)

delta (n)

desert (n)

ocean (n)

range (n)

the Antarctic (n)

the Arctic (n)

the North Pole (n)

the South Pole (n)

the Tropics (n)

tropical (adj)

THEME 6
Culture and Civilization, That's Terrible!

bride (n)

ceremony (n)

get married (v)

groom (n)

marriage (n)

wedding (n)

bury (v)

condolences (n)

cremate (v)

cremation (n)

funeral (n)

grave (n)

wreath (n)

THEME 7
They Made Our World, Liquid Crystals

answer (phone) (v)

call (v)

dial (v)

engaged (adj)

extension (n)

free (adj)

hang up (v)

hold (line) (v)

pick up (v)

put through (v)

switchboard (n)

telephonist (n)

tone (n)

calculator (n)

circuit board (n)

component (n)

crystal (n)

device (n)

digital (n)

display (n and v)

pass through (v)

signal (n)

THEME 8
Art and Literature, Sindbad the Sailor

borrow (v)

cut (v)

fall (v)

hear (v)

hand (give to) (v)

hurt (v)

knock (v)

lie (v)

look (appear) (v)

realise (v)

return (give back) (v)

see (v)

think (v)

wait (v)

catch (v)

drop (v)

fantasy (n)

fly (v)

legend (n)

legendary (adj)

myth (n)

mythical (adj)

remember (v)

sink (v)

swim (v)

(un)tie (v)

trap (v)

work out (v)

THEME 9
Sports and Leisure,
Where Shall We Go?

board (n)

go (n)

in turns

land on (v)

opponent (n)

piece (n)

spinner (n)

square (n)

track (n)

turn (n)

attraction (n)

cost (v)

destination (n)

domestic (adj)

equipment (n)

season (n)

tourist (n)

transfer (n)

travel agent (n)

view (n)

THEME 10
Nutrition and Health,
More Truths and Myths

arm (n)

body (n)

ear (n)

eye (n)

face (n)

foot (n)

hair (n)

hand (n)

leg (n)

mouth (n)

nose (n)

skin (n)

teeth (n)

tooth (n)

ache (n)

bone (n)

calorie (n)

digestion (n)

disease (n)

energy (n)

exercise (n)

fat (adj and n)

fit (adj)

heart (n)

hip (n)

lung (n)

medicine (n)

muscle (n)

stomach (n)

waist (n)

ache (n)

adapt (v)

alternative (n)

amphibian (n)

angry (adj)

animal (n)

answer (phone) (v)

apologise (v)

area (n)

argue (v)

argument (n)

arm (n)

attraction (n)

aural (adj)

backbone (n)

behave (v)

board (n)

body (n)

bone (n)

borrow (v)

bride (n)

bury (v)

calculator (n)

call (v)

calm (adj)

calorie (n)

carbon (n)

catch (v)

cause (n)

ceremony (n)

change (mind) (v)

choose (v)

circuit board (n)

climate (n)

cold-blooded (adj)

colleague (n)

component (n)

concentrate (v)

concentration (n)

condolences (n)

conflict (n)

convert (v)

cost (v)

cremate (v)

cremation (n)

crystal (n)

cut (v)

cycle (n)

deal with (v)

decide (v)

decision (n)

delta (n)

desert (n)

destination (n)

device (n)

dial (v)

digestion (n)

digital (n)

discussion (n)

disease (n)

dismiss (v)

display (n and v)

distract (v)

domestic (adj)

drop (v)

ear (n)

energy (n)

engaged (adj)

equipment *(n)*

exercise *(n)*

extension *(n)*

eye *(n)*

face *(n)*

fall *(v)*

fantasy *(n)*

fat *(adj and n)*

feather *(n)*

fit *(adj)*

fly *(v)*

foot *(n)*

free *(adj)*

funeral *(n)*

fur *(n)*

gas *(n)*

get married *(v)*

go *(n)*

grave *(n)*

groom *(n)*

hair *(n)*

hand (give to) *(v)*

hand *(n)*

handle *(v)*

hang up *(v)*

hear *(v)*

heart *(n)*

hip *(n)*

hold (line) *(v)*

hurt *(v)*

hydrogen *(n)*

ignore *(v)*

in turns

insect *(n)*

involve *(v)*

kinaesthetic *(adj)*

knock *(v)*

land on *(v)*

learner *(n)*

leg *(n)*

legend *(n)*

legendary *(adj)*

lie *(v)*

liquid *(n)*

location *(n)*

look (appear) *(v)*

lung *(n)*

make up (mind) *(v)*

mammal *(n)*

management *(n)*

manager *(n)*

marriage *(n)*

matter *(n and v)*

medicine *(n)*

mode *(n)*

mouth *(n)*

muscle *(n)*

myth *(n)*

mythical *(adj)*

nitrogen *(n)*

nose *(n)*

ocean *(n)*

opponent *(n)*

organisation *(n)*

organise *(v)*

oxygen *(n)*

pass through *(v)*

pick up *(v)*

piece *(n)*

plant *(n)*

point *(n)*

population *(n)*

process *(n)*

project *(n)*

put through *(v)*

range *(n)*

realise *(v)*

region *(n)*

regret *(n and v)*

remember *(v)*

reptile *(n)*

research *(n)*

return (give back) *(v)*

role play *(n)*

scale *(n)*

season *(n)*

see *(v)*

signal *(n)*

sink *(v)*

skin *(n)*

solid *(n)*

sorry *(adj)*

spinner *(n)*

square *(n)*

stomach *(n)*

suppose *(v)*

swim *(v)*

switchboard *(n)*

teeth *(n)*

telephonist *(n)*

temperature *(n)*

the Antarctic *(n)*

the Arctic *(n)*

the North Pole *(n)*

the South Pole *(n)*

the Tropics *(n)*

(un)tie *(v)*

think *(v)*

TO DO list *(n)*

tone *(n)*

tooth *(n)*

tourist *(n)*

track *(n)*

transfer *(n)*

trap *(v)*

travel agent *(n)*

tropical *(adj)*

turn *(n)*

upset *(adj)*

urgent *(adj)*

view *(n)*

visual *(adj)*

waist *(n)*

wait *(v)*

warm-blooded *(adj)*

wedding *(n)*

work out *(v)*

worker *(n)*

wreath *(n)*

wrong *(adj)*

Tapescript

Presenter: **Theme 1: Education, It's Not My Style**
Lesson 1: Vocabulary
C Read and listen to the text. Complete it with a green word or phrase in each space. Make any necessary changes.

Voice: What activities are you looking forward to in this theme? Do you like exercises that involve pairwork? Or do you prefer discussions in small groups? What about a role play, where you take the part of a different person and act out a scene?
Everybody has a learning style. Some people don't see the point in crosswords and puzzles, while others learn a lot by working things out in this way. What about you? Some people love research, in the library or on the Internet, while others prefer to be told the important information in a lecture. Which type of person are you? My personal favourite is the *project* that involves making something. I suppose that's because I'm a kinaesthetic learner.

Presenter: **Lesson 2: Speaking**
A 3 Listen and check.

Voice: neat
career
psychologist
screen
convert
restless
gestures
layout

Presenter: **Lesson 3: Checking skills**
A 1 Listen to each pair of words or phrases.

Voice:
a	physical	visual
b	text	ticks it
c	screen	scare Ian
d	rings	ring his
e	career	crier
f	the things	the thing is
g	I can do it.	I can't do it.
h	That sounds good.	That sound is good.
i	It provides good support.	It provides good sport.

Presenter: **B 5 Listen and check.**
Voice: angina
barge
consign
gen
ginger
glade
goad
insignia
thorough

Presenter: **Lesson 4: Applying skills**
A 2 Listen and check.
Voice: Column 1
making
name
play
say
they

Column 2
pair
their
there
wear
where

Column 3
assignment
designer
find
require
typing

Column 4
go
know
most
role
so

Column 5
about
allowed
around
out
sound

Column 6
career
clear
engineer
hear
idea

Presenter: **Theme 2: Daily Life, Are You a Maximizer or a Satisficer?**
Lesson 1: Vocabulary
C 2 Listen and check your answers.

Voice: Imagine that you are offered two jobs. Both jobs are interesting. The money is good in both cases. How would you choose between them? How would you decide which job to take?
Mary Orwell had this problem. She made a decision quite quickly. She thought about the two alternatives for a few days and then chose one. She is not sure now that this was the best decision, but she is not unhappy about it. She has no regrets at all. 'There is only one thing worse than a bad decision,' she says, 'and that is no decision at all.'
Mary's friend, Fleur Arnold, had the same problem, but she behaved in a different way. She thought about the alternatives for a long time, getting more and more information about each job. Finally, she made up her mind. She didn't phone the company, though. She waited for a few more days … and changed her mind. She still didn't accept the job, and finally she changed her mind again and chose the first job. However, she was not happy with her decision. 'I think the other job was better,' she says now.

Presenter: **Lesson 2: Speaking**
A 2 Listen and check your ideas.
Mary: Hi, Fleur. Do you want a coffee?
Fleur: I'm not sure.
Mary: Go on. I'm having one.
Fleur: OK. I'll have one then.

Mary:	What kind do you want? Cappuccino, latte, americano, espresso …
Fleur:	Stop! Too many choices!
Mary:	What do you mean? Choice is good. I love having lots of choices.
Fleur:	I don't. The more choices I have, the harder it is to make a decision.

Presenter: **C Listen to the second part of the conversation between Mary and Fleur. Complete this summary of the article.**

Mary:	That's a coincidence.
Fleur:	What is?
Mary:	You said you find it hard to make decisions. I read a really interesting article about decision-making the other day.
Fleur:	Great. Perhaps it can help me. What did it say?
Mary:	Well, apparently, there are two kinds of people, *maximizers* and *satisficers*.
Fleur:	You mean *satisfiers*?
Mary:	No, I'm sure it said *satisficers*.
Fleur:	Oh, OK.
Mary:	It seems that maximizers are always unhappy with their decisions.
Fleur:	Just like me. But why?
Mary:	Because they always think there was a better alternative.
Fleur:	That *does* sound like me. And what about satisfiers?
Mary:	*Ficers.*
Fleur:	Whatever.
Mary:	Well, as I understand it, satisficers make decisions easily because they just want something that is good enough. They are happier in their daily life because they don't regret decisions.
Fleur:	That's fascinating.

Presenter: **D Listen to the final part of the conversation. Answer the questions.**

Fleur:	Who said all this?
Mary:	I can't remember.
Fleur:	Well, where did you read about it?
Mary:	I don't know. Some newspaper.
Fleur:	So which book does all this appear in?
Mary:	I've no idea.
Fleur:	Oh, Mary! You're hopeless. When you read something interesting, you must make a note of names and publications and so on.
Mary:	Sorry. I'll get the coffee.
Fleur:	Hang on! I haven't decided yet.

Presenter: **Lesson 3: Learning new skills**
A 2 Listen and check your ideas.

Voice:	behave	behaviour
	believe	belief
	choose	choice
	decide	decision
	maximize	maximum
	produce	product
	regret	regret
	research	research
	satisfy	satisfaction
	solve	solution

Presenter: **B 2 Listen and check your ideas.**

Voice:	a In 1947, an American economist and social scientist called Herbert Simon coined these terms in his book *Administrative Behavior*.

b He claimed that there are two kinds of decision-maker. *Maximizers* cannot make decisions easily because there are often good alternatives.

c *Satisficers*, on the other hand, make up their minds quite quickly because they are just looking for something that satisfies their needs.

d Does it matter if you are a maximizer or a satisficer? According to Simon, it does. His research showed that people who are maximizers are often dissatisfied with life, while satisficers are not.

Presenter: **Lesson 4: Applying new skills**
A 3 Listen and check your ideas.

Voice:	a There are often a number of alternatives.
	b You are already in a lot of trouble.
	c What an awful old umbrella!
	d We all agree about the exam answers.
	e I don't know if I'll ever ask you again.

Presenter: **Theme 3: Work and Business, The Person and the Problem**
Lesson 1: Vocabulary
C Read and listen to the article. Complete it with a green word in each space. Make any necessary changes.

Voice: The dictionary defines conflict as 'a fight or struggle between two people or two groups of people'. There are conflict situations at home between husbands and wives and parents and children. There are conflict situations at school among students or between students and teachers. There are conflict situations at work, among workers or between workers and managers. Charles Handy, the British writer on management, believes we all need to know how to handle conflict, not just in business but in our own social lives, too. In his book *Understanding Organisations* (1985), he writes: 'An understanding of the possible sources of conflict and the strategies for handling conflict are essential to effective management in organisations and even to individual survival.'

In other words, Handy believes we need to understand the possible causes of conflict and how to deal with it, as a manager in an organisation and as a person in daily life. If we are slow at dealing with conflict, the results can be very bad. A manager may dismiss a worker, a child may leave home, husbands and wives may separate.

How do *you* handle conflict? Do you get angry and start an argument? Do you get upset? Or do you try to ignore the problem and hope that it will go away? What is the best way to behave?

Presenter: **Lesson 2: Speaking**
A Read and listen to the case study on the right. What problem must you deal with in this case?

Voice: You are the manager of a small company called Allen's Construction. For years you worked with a small group of colleagues, but last month the previous manager left and you were offered the job. You accepted and the other workers were happy. At least, all of them were except Andreas. At first, when you asked him to do something, he often ignored your instructions. Then he started to argue every time. Just after lunch yesterday, you gave him a job to do and he shouted, 'Do it yourself. You shouldn't be the manager anyway. You only got the job because you are Mr. Allen's cousin.' Then he stormed out and went home. He has

just arrived at work this morning. It seems that he has forgotten the argument.
What should you do?

Presenter: **F Read and listen to the article from Management Today.**

Voice: In their book, *Developing Management Skills*, David Whetten and Kim Cameron talk about separating the person and the problem. They point out that people are not problems. People have problems. When there is conflict, it is easy to attack the person, not the problem. You say things like:
You are stupid.
You are always late.
You are lazy.
This is a mistake. Try not to use the verb *be* in an argument. We use *be* in statements of fact, to describe fixed or long-term situations, like *You are French* or *You are eighteen*. If you use *You are …* about a person's behaviour, it sounds like the person can never change.
Concentrate instead on **what** happened:
You forgot to give me the message.
You arrived late three times last week.
You didn't finish the work that I gave you.
Talk only about actions. Don't mention facts or ideas that are not relevant. Then try to find out **why** the action happened *and* **how** to stop it happening again.

Presenter: **Lesson 3: Learning new skills**
B 2 Listen and check your ideas.

Voice: Are you for or against?
Do it yourself.
I always work hard.
I saw a man.
I'd like more of those.
They all accepted.
We often go there.
Who opened the door?
You asked me.

Presenter: **Theme 4: Science and Nature, Adapting to the Climate**
Lesson 2: Speaking
B 1 Read and listen to the text.

Voice: How do animals survive in very cold or very hot climates? Over thousands of years, the animals we see today at the poles and in the desert have adapted to temperatures below -80°C and above 50°C. There are three main ways in which animals have adapted:
• behaviour – they behave in a particular way
• physical features – size or shape of body or parts of it
• body functions – their organs work in a particular way

Presenter: **Lesson 3: Learning new skills**
A 3 Listen to the pairs of words.

Voice:
a hibernate   hibernation
b adapt   adaptation
c identify   identification
d insulate   insulation
e classify   classification
f migrate   migration
g condense   condensation
h evaporate   evaporation

Presenter: **C Read and listen to the conversation.**
A: In winter, the wood frog goes into hibernation.
B: What does *hibernation* mean?
A: It means the animal stops breathing and the heart stops.
B: Why do animals … what's the verb?
A: Hibernate.
B: How do you pronounce it?
A: '*Hibernate*. Stress the first syllable.
B: Why do animals hibernate?
A: Because there is not enough food.
B: I see. Carry on.
A: Well, the frog's blood falls below freezing point. But the blood doesn't actually freeze.
B: Why not?
A: Because the frog has a special chemical in its blood.
B: Sorry. I don't understand the part about the blood.
A: The frog produces a kind of antifreeze – like in a car engine.
B: Oh, right.

Presenter: **Theme 5: The Physical World, Do You Know Your Region?**
Lesson 1: Vocabulary
B 2 Listen and check your answers.

Voice: Around the centre of the Earth there is an imaginary line. We call it the Equator because there is equal area to the north and to the south of the line. The area on either side of the Equator is called the Tropics. The weather here is tropical, which means it is very hot and often very wet. At the very north of the Earth, we find the North Pole. The area around the North Pole is called the Arctic. At the very south of the Earth, we find the South Pole. The area around the South Pole is called the Antarctic.

Presenter: **C 2 Listen and check your answers.**
Voice 1: 1 The largest continent in the world is Asia, with an area of 44 million km^2.
Voice 2: 2 The largest country in the world is Russia, with an area of 17 million km^2.
Voice 3: 3 The wettest place in the world is Cherranpunji, India, with average rainfall of 1,270 cm p.a.
Voice 1: 4 The driest place in the world is the Atacama Desert in Chile in South America, with less than 0.01 cm p.a.
Voice 2: 5 The hottest place in the world is El Azizia, Libya, with a highest ever temperature of 57.8°C.
Voice 3: 6 The coldest place in the world is the South Pole, with a lowest ever temperature of –89.4°C.
Voice 1: 7 The largest desert in the world is the Sahara, with an area of 8.5 million km^2.
Voice 2: 8 The largest ocean in the world is the Pacific, with an area of 166 million km^2.
Voice 3: 9 The largest island in the world is Australia, with an area of 7.6 million km^2.
Voice 1: 10 The largest lake in the world is the Caspian Sea, Iran, with an area of 371,000 km^2.
Voice 2: 11 The longest mountain range is the Andes, South America, which is 7,200 km long.
Voice 3: 12 The highest mountain in the world is Mount Everest, which is 8,848 metres high.
Voice 1: 13 The longest river in the world is the Nile, which is 6,670 km long.
Voice 2: 14 The biggest river in the world is the Amazon, which has a delta with an area of 7 million km^2.
Voice 3: 15 The lowest point in the world is the Dead Sea, Jordan, which is 395 metres below sea level.

Presenter: Lesson 2: Speaking
A 2 Listen and check your answers.

Voice: lakes
seas
mountains
rivers
oceans
deserts
islands
countries

Presenter: **B 2 Listen to the first part of the talk and check your answers.**

Voice: I come from the continent of North America. *[pause]*
The continent stretches from the Tropics in the south to the Arctic Ocean in the north. It is bordered by the North Atlantic Ocean in the east and the North Pacific Ocean in the west. *[pause]*
People often think of North America as simply the United States, and perhaps Canada, but in fact there are 24 countries on the continent, including Mexico and Cuba, a large island off the southeast coast of the United States. *[pause]*
The continent has two main mountain ranges. In the east are the Appalachians and in the west the Rockies. However, the highest point on the continent is not in the Appalachians or the Rockies. Instead, it is Mount McKinley, in the northwest of the continent. The mountain rises over 6,000 metres. *[pause]*
There are many large rivers, including the St Lawrence and the Colorado, but the longest is the Mississippi-Missouri, which rises in the north of the United States and flows out of the Mississippi Delta into the Gulf of Mexico. The river is over 4,000 kilometres long. *[pause]*
There are also many large lakes, including the series called the Great Lakes, on the border between the United States and Canada. *[pause]*
There are several deserts in the southwest of the United States, including the Mojave. This desert contains the famous Death Valley, which is the hottest and driest location on the continent. *[pause]*
There are many islands on the continent, including the West Indies, which is a large group of islands off the southwest coast of the United States. The West Indies are surrounded by the Caribbean Sea. *[pause]*
The largest island on the continent is Greenland, in the extreme northeast. In fact, some people call this the world's largest island, because they say that Australia is a country, not an island. *[pause]*

Presenter: **D 2 Listen to the first part of the talk again and check or correct your labels.**
[REPEAT OF LESSON 3 EXERCISE B2]

Presenter: **E 2 Listen to the last part of the talk about North America. Write the colour of each climate region in the space provided.**

Voice: North America is the only continent with all the climate types in the world.
As you can see from the map, in the far north we have the Arctic type, then the subarctic. Most of Canada has a tundra climate – that's the dark blue part – with low temperatures and no rainfall all year round. There are no trees. The eastern side of the United States – here – has a humid climate in the north, which means hot wet summers, and a humid subtropical climate in the south, which means very hot, wet summers. That's

the orange part here. Most of the western side of the United States has a subtropical climate, dry and hot, with a large area of desert climate (the red part here), which is of course dry and very hot. Central America, in the Tropics here, has a wet tropical climate.

Presenter: Lesson 4: Applying new skills
C Listen to a more detailed version of the talk from Lesson 2. Check your notes. Make more notes for other headings.

Voice: I come from the continent of North America. *[pause]*
The continent stretches from the Tropics in the south to the Arctic Ocean in the north. It is bordered by the North Atlantic Ocean in the east and the North Pacific Ocean in the west. *[pause]*
People often think of North America as simply the United States, and perhaps Canada, but in fact there are 24 countries on the continent, including Mexico and Cuba, a large island off the southeast coast of the United States. *[pause]*
The largest country in the continent by area is Canada. It is nearly 10 million square kilometres. The United States is a little smaller, at just over nine million square kilometres. *[pause]*
However, the United States is much bigger than Canada in terms of population. The country has more than 250 million people, compared with Canada's 27 million. *[pause]*
The smallest country on the continent is called St Kitts and Nevis. That's S-T K-I-double-T-S and N-E-V-I-S. It comprises two islands, with a total area of just 269 square kilometres. *[pause]*
St Kitts and Nevis is also the smallest country in terms of population, with only 38,000 inhabitants. *[pause]*
The continent has two main mountain ranges. In the east are the Appalachians and in the west the Rockies. However, the highest point on the continent is not in the Appalachians or the Rockies. Instead, it is Mount McKinley, in the northwest of the continent. The mountain rises over 6,000 metres. *[pause]*
There are many large rivers, including the St Lawrence – that's S-T L-A-W-R-E-N-C-E and the Colorado – C-O-L-O-R-A-D-O, but the longest is the Mississippi-Missouri, which rises in the north of the United States and flows out of the Mississippi Delta into the Gulf of Mexico. The river is over 4,000 kilometres long. *[pause]*
There are also many large lakes, including the series called the Great Lakes, on the border between the United States and Canada. The largest lake is called Lake Superior. It is over 80,000 square kilometres. *[pause]*
There are several deserts in the southwest of the United States, including the Mojave. This desert contains the famous Death Valley, which is the hottest and driest location on the continent. Temperatures in Death Valley have reached 50 degrees centigrade. There is sometimes less than four centimetres of rain in one year. Death Valley is also the lowest point on the continent, at minus 86 metres, that is 86 metres below sea level. *[pause]*
The wettest parts of the continent are in the northwest of the United States, near the border with Canada. This area has average rainfall of nearly 400 centimetres per year. *[pause]*
There are many islands on the continent, including the West Indies, which is a large group of islands off the southwest coast of the United States. The West Indies are surrounded by the Caribbean Sea. *[pause]*

The largest island on the continent is Greenland, in the extreme northeast. In fact, some people call this the world's largest island, because they say that Australia is a country, not an island. Greenland belongs to the European country Denmark. It has an area of more than 2 million square kilometres. The coldest place on the continent is in Greenland at North Ice, in the north of the island. *[pause]*

Presenter: **Theme 6: Culture and Civilization, That's Terrible!**
Lesson 1: Vocabulary
C Read and listen to the text.

Voice: Nobody likes to give bad news. Perhaps this is why in English we give bad news in an indirect way. Firstly, we usually introduce the news. We say, 'I'm afraid I've got some really bad news,' or 'I've got something to tell you.' The second sentence could mean *any* kind of news, but it always means *bad* news. Then we introduce the topic – 'It's about John,' or 'You remember John, don't you?' Perhaps we give some background information – 'He was swimming in the sea the other day.' By now, the other person has probably guessed, but we still don't give the information directly. Instead of saying 'He's dead,' we say 'He's passed away.'
Some indirect ways of speaking are called *euphemisms*. There are euphemisms for most kinds of bad news. For example, if you get fired, you tell people, 'I lost my job' or 'They let me go.'
Sometimes there is no special euphemism. We just avoid using the positive verb. For example, we don't say, 'You failed the exam.' Instead, we say, 'You didn't pass.'

Presenter: **Lesson 2: Speaking**
A Alan and Gopal are talking about their latest speaking assignment. Listen to the first part of their conversation.

Alan: So what are you going to talk about?
Gopal: I'm not sure. I can talk about my own country, can't I?
Alan: That's right.
Gopal: But we must compare two countries, mustn't we?
Alan: I think so. So you can compare your country with another country. You come from India, don't you?
Gopal: Yes. My home city is Mumbai.
Alan: That was once Bombay, wasn't it?
Gopal: That's right. Are you going to talk about your country?
Alan: I haven't decided yet … Oh, by the way, I'm afraid I've got some really bad news …

Presenter: **B Listen to the second part of the conversation.**
Gopal: What is it?
Alan: It's about David.
Gopal: What about him?
Alan: He was in a road accident the other day.
Gopal: Really? What happened?
Alan: I don't know all the details. I think he was crossing the main road near the traffic lights.
Gopal: Is he all right?
Alan: No, he didn't make it.
Gopal: What do you mean?
Alan: I mean they couldn't save him.
Gopal: You mean, he's dead?
Alan: Yes.
Gopal: How awful!
Alan: Yes. They got him to the hospital, but he passed away a few hours later.
Gopal: That's terrible!

Alan: I know. It's tragic.
Gopal: What a dreadful thing to happen!

Presenter: **C 2 Listen to the third part.**
Alan: The funeral's on Friday.
Gopal: The what?
Alan: The funeral. A funeral is the ceremony when we bury someone.
Gopal: *Bury* means *put in the ground,* doesn't it?
Alan: Yes. In a grave. Do you know the word *grave*?
Gopal: I think so. A grave is a hole in the ground, isn't it?
Alan: That's right.
Gopal: Are you going to the … ah … funeral?
Alan: Yes, I am.
Gopal: Will you give the family my … what's the word?
Alan: Condolences.
Gopal: Condo …
Alan: … lences
Gopal: Condolences.
Alan: Yes, of course I will. Do you want to send some flowers?
Gopal: You only send flowers for weddings, don't you?
Alan: No, actually, we send flowers for funerals, too. Often we send a wreath.
Gopal: What's a wreath?
Alan: It's flowers or leaves in a ring.
Gopal: R-E-E-T-H?
Alan: No, it's wreath. The W is silent. W-R-E-A-T-H.
Gopal: OK. I will send a … wreath with my … condolences to the … funeral.
Alan: You cremate people in your culture, don't you?
Gopal: Does cremate mean to burn a body?
Alan: Yes, it does.
Gopal: Then, yes, we do. We … sorry, what was the word?
Alan: Cremate.
Gopal: How do you spell it?
Alan: C-R-E-M-A-T-E.
Gopal: 'Cremate.
Alan: No, cre'mate.
Gopal: OK. We cremate people. We throw the … what do you call the thing that is left after burning?
Alan: The ashes.
Gopal: Oh, yes. The ashes. We throw the ashes in the river. In the Ganges, if possible.

Presenter: **D 2 Listen to the third part again.**
[REPEAT OF LESSON 2 EXERCISE C2]

Presenter: **Lesson 3: Learning new skills**
A 5 Listen and check your answers.
1
Alan: So what are you going to talk about?
Gopal: I'm not sure. I can talk about my own country, can't I?
Alan: That's right.
Gopal: But we must compare two countries, mustn't we?
Alan: I think so. So you can compare your country with another country. You come from India, don't you?
Gopal: Yes. My home city is Mumbai.
Alan: That was once Bombay, wasn't it?
Gopal: That's right.

Presenter: **2**
Alan: A funeral is the ceremony when we bury someone.
Gopal: *Bury* means *put in the ground*, doesn't it?
Alan: Yes. In a grave. Do you know the word *grave*?
Gopal: I think so. A grave is a hole in the ground, isn't it?

Presenter:	**3**	
Alan:	Do you want to send some flowers?	
Gopal:	You only send flowers for weddings, don't you?	
Alan:	No, actually, we send flowers for funerals, too.	

Presenter: **4**

Alan: You cremate people in your culture, don't you?
Gopal: Yes, we do.

Presenter: **C 2 Listen to the sentences again.**
[REPEAT OF LESSON 3 EXERCISE A5]

Presenter: **Lesson 4: Applying new skills**
C 2 Listen and check your answers.
Voice: In the culture of Britain and North America there are several customs associated with death. There is always a funeral, which is a ceremony, usually in a church. There are often lots of flowers, especially wreaths, from people who have sent their condolences to the family. After the service, most people are buried in a grave, but sometimes people are cremated, and their ashes are buried or spread in a place that was special to the person.

Presenter: **Theme 7: They Made Our World, Liquid Crystals**
Lesson 1: Vocabulary
B Read and listen to the text. Write a green word or phrase in each space. Make any necessary changes.
Voice: There are three states of matter: solid, liquid and gas. Water can exist in all three states. Sugar can exist as a solution (or liquid) and as crystals (or solid). If you leave a sugar solution in the bottom of a cup, the water evaporates and leaves sugar crystals.
Some substances, however, can exist as a liquid and a solid at the same time. They are called liquid crystals. Liquid crystals look like solids, but when you send an electrical signal to them, they become liquids. Light can pass through the solid crystals, but it cannot pass through the liquid crystals.
The most common use for liquid crystals is the LCD, or liquid-crystal display. The LCD is a component in your mobile phone, your digital watch and your pocket calculator and in many other electronic devices. It displays a number when it receives a signal from the circuit board.

Presenter: **Lesson 3: Learning new skills**
A Listen to and read the text. Look at Figure 2.
Voice: You can display all the numbers 0 to 9 on a seven-rectangle LCD, for example, on a pocket calculator. You can also display some of the capital letters in English, but not all of them. For the LCD of a mobile phone, you need to add an extra six rectangles, so when you press, for example, A, the letter appears on the display (see Figure 2).

Presenter: **Theme 8: Art and Literature, Sindbad the Sailor**
Lesson 1: Vocabulary
Narrator: Joha and the Donkey
One day, Ali, Joha's neighbour, came to Joha's house and asked to borrow his donkey for the day.
'Of course,' said Joha, and Ali took it away. Joha waited, but he didn't bring it back, so Joha went round to see him.
'Can I have my donkey back, please?' asked Joha.
'I'm sorry,' said the man. 'I'm afraid your donkey isn't here, but he'll be back tomorrow.'

So Joha went round to his neighbour's house the following day and asked for the donkey again.
'I'm so sorry,' said the other man. 'My son took it to town, but he'll come back this evening.'
Just then, Joha's donkey brayed in the neighbour's back garden! Joha was very angry.
'Neighbour! I'm surprised at you. You said my donkey isn't here, but I heard it bray in your back garden.'
The other man looked angry.
'Joha. I'm surprised at you. How long have we known each other? Do you believe your neighbour or your donkey?'

Presenter: **A 2 Listen and check your answers.**
Narrator: Joha and the Tree
One day, Joha's neighbour, Ali, heard a strange sound. He went out into his garden and saw Joha up a tree. He was cutting a branch. Ali realised immediately that Joha was cutting the branch that he was sitting on.
'Be careful, Joha,' he said. 'That branch will fall and you'll hurt yourself badly.'
Joha did not take any notice, but a few seconds later, he cut through the wood and the branch fell to the ground. Joha fell, too, and hurt himself badly. He lay on the ground. He thought, 'It is amazing. My neighbour said the branch would fall and it fell. He said I would hurt myself badly and I hurt myself badly.'
He got up and knocked on his neighbour's door. When Ali answered it, Joha said, 'Wise neighbour, you can see the future. Tell me. When will I die?'

Presenter: **B 3 Listen and number the pictures in order.**
Narrator: Sindbad was a sailor. He was trapped on a desert island. His ship had sunk and he had swum to the shore. There were no trees, no bushes and no animals on the island. There was nothing to eat at all, and Sindbad couldn't get off. *[pause]*
He found a large, white ball. He realised that it was a roc's egg. The roc was a huge mythical creature. Sindbad tried to open the egg, but the shell was too hard to break. *[pause]*
Just then, he heard a noise and looked up. He saw a huge bird coming down towards him. The roc had a snake in its mouth. Sindbad worked out that the bird had caught the snake on another island. *[pause]*
Sindbad hid near the egg. The bird sat on the egg and Sindbad tied himself to its leg. *[pause]*
When the bird flew off in the morning to find food, it carried Sindbad high into the sky. He was terrified. Finally, the bird arrived at a deep valley. Sindbad untied himself from the bird's leg and dropped to the ground. He found a lot of diamonds all around him. Sindbad remembered the legend of the Valley of Diamonds.

Presenter: **B 4 Listen again and write the green verbs next to each picture.**
[REPEAT OF LESSON 1 EXERCISE B3]

Presenter: **Lesson 2: Speaking**
C Listen to Afet and Karli. They are talking about traditional stories.
[Note: // = markings for pausing on second playing]
Afet: Have you heard the story of Sindbad and the Valley of Diamonds?
Karli: I don't think so. How does it go? //
Afet: Well, Sindbad was in the legendary Valley of Diamonds …
Karli: How did he get there?

Afet:	Well, it's a long story.
Karli:	Just give me a synopsis.
Afet:	A what?
Karli:	A brief summary of the story.
Afet:	OK. His ship had sunk and he'd swum to a desert island. He'd found the egg of a roc.
Karli:	The egg of a what?
Afet:	A roc. //
Karli:	How do you spell it?
Afet:	R-O-C. It's a mythical bird. The roc had come back with a snake in its mouth, and Sindbad had hidden behind the egg. He'd …
Karli:	Hang on a minute. What's the significance of the snake? //
Afet:	Ah, well, you see, Sindbad hadn't seen any animals on the island. So he'd worked out that the bird had visited another place to find food. So he'd tied himself to the roc's leg …
Karli:	He'd done what?
Afet:	Tied himself to the roc's leg, and the next day …
Karli:	How had he tied himself to the bird's leg?
Afet:	It doesn't matter how he'd tied himself. // With his turban, maybe.
Karli:	His turban? What's that?
Afet:	It's a piece of cloth that you wear around your head. Anyway, the bird had carried him to the Valley of Diamonds.
Karli:	The snakes lived there, didn't they?
Afet:	Yes, I suppose so. //
Karli:	But he couldn't eat the snakes, could he? So why did he want to go there?
Afet:	It's just a legend. A legend is a story with strange creatures and fantastic events.
Karli:	It's ridiculous.
Afet:	Why?
Karli:	Because in real life, the bird would feel him on its leg.
Afet:	It might not feel him. //
Karli:	OK, but even if it didn't feel him, it couldn't fly with a man tied to its leg.
Afet:	Well, it's only a story. Look, do you want to hear about the Valley of Diamonds or not?
Karli:	Yes, sure. I was only saying that …

Presenter:	**D 2 Listen again and check your answers.** [REPEAT OF LESSON 2 EXERCISE C]

Presenter:	**Theme 9: Sports and Leisure, Where Shall We Go?** **Lesson 1: Vocabulary** **C Pablo and Pierre are discussing holidays.** **1 Listen to their conversation. Tick any of your questions that you hear.**
Pablo:	Let's go on holiday together this year. I'd really like to go to Lakes End.
Pierre:	Where is it?
Pablo:	It's in Patagonia.
Pierre:	And where's *that*?
Pablo:	It's in my country, Argentina. Lakes End is actually on the western shore of Lake La Plata.
Pierre:	Is that near the Atacama Desert?
Pablo:	No. The Atacama is much further north.
Pierre:	How do you get to Lakes End?
Pablo:	Ah, now, that's a slight problem. First, you fly to Buenos Aires and then you take an internal flight to the town of Comodoro Rivadavia …
Pierre:	Sorry. *What's* the name of the town?
Pablo:	Comodoro Rivadavia.
Pierre:	That sounds like a long journey.

Pablo:	Wait. I haven't finished yet. Then you go in a four-by-four to Lake La Plata, then you go by motorboat to Lakes End.
Pierre:	So it's a long way from civilization?
Pablo:	Yes, it is. It's probably one of the remotest places on Earth.
Pierre:	Where can you stay?
Pablo:	In a log cabin.
Pierre:	What can you see there?
Pablo:	Well, there is no daily contact with other people, but there are beautiful views of the Andes Mountains.
Pierre:	*What* are the mountains called?
Pablo:	The Andes. They run from the south of South America right up the Pacific Ocean coast.
Pierre:	How much does it cost?
Pablo:	$1,500 per person for eight nights.
Pierre:	Does that include all the flights and the four-wheel drive and so on?
Pablo:	Yes, all the travel, or 'transfers' as the travel agent calls them. But you have to buy food and cook it yourself.
Pierre:	When is the best time to go?
Pablo:	There isn't really a tourist season. You can go any time of the year, but the weather is cold in winter and very warm in summer.
Pierre:	What should you take – I mean, do you need special clothes or equipment?
Pablo:	Well, you just need suitable clothes for the time of year. As for equipment, you should take a good pair of walking boots, a fishing rod … oh, and lots of books.
Pierre:	So there aren't many tourist attractions.
Pablo:	None. You just see nature in its original form, before Man arrived to spoil things. So do you want to go?
Pierre:	I don't know. I like nature and walking and fishing … and reading, of course. But I'd prefer to go somewhere a bit closer to civilization. It sounds a bit scary.
Pablo:	I don't think it's scary. It's … natural.
Pierre:	Mmm. I'd rather go to a place with a few other people.
Pablo:	OK. So Lakes End is not the right sort of holiday for you.

Presenter:	**C 2 Listen again. Complete Table 1 with notes of the key information.** [REPEAT OF LESSON 1 EXERCISE C1]

Presenter:	**Lesson 3: Learning new skills** **B Listen to the people above discussing the holidays from Lesson 2.**
A:	So, we could go diving in the Amazon, we could fly a Russian jet plane, stay in a Swedish icehouse or go cycling and hiking on the Italian coast. We've got four choices.
B:	No, five. Don't forget fishing in the Argentinian lake.
A:	Oh, yes, of course. Well, I think that we should all give an opinion and then I suggest that we vote.
B:	Fair enough. But I think you should be the chairperson, Pierre.
A:	Why do we need a chairperson?
B:	Someone has to make sure that everyone has a say.
A:	OK. Shall I be the chairperson? … OK. Let's start with you, then, Adam. Where do *you* think we should go?
B:	Well, I would like to go to Argentina. I think the lake sounds fantastic.
C:	Do you really? I would prefer to do something a bit more exciting. The Russian plane sounds incredible.
D:	Yes, well, perhaps that's a little *too* exciting! I'd rather go somewhere with beautiful views, like the lake …
C:	And the jet plane …

D: Yes, I suppose so. But I was going to say beautiful views and interesting people – and of course wonderful food.

C: You mean hiking and cycling on the Italian coast?

D: Exactly. I love Italy, and that is a wonderful way to really see the country.

A: Any more suggestions? Carlos. We haven't heard from you yet.

E: I don't really mind, as long as it's not the jet plane. That sounds terrifying.

A: Would anyone else like to say anything? … So, shall we vote on it? …
Hands up all those in favour of the diving holiday. Thank you. And all those against. …
OK. So that's three votes for the icehouse, two for the jet fighter and one for the lake. That's a bit of a problem.

B: May I make a suggestion?

A: Yes, of course.

B: I suggest that we eliminate the lake, because it came last, and vote again.

A: OK. Let's vote again …
I'm afraid it's a tie now. Three votes for the icehouse, three for the jet fighter.

B: I think we are forgetting something. The jet fighter costs $10,000 per person. I can't possibly afford that.

A: True, true. So it's the icehouse, is it?

B: I think it has to be.

Presenter: **C 3 Listen and check.**

A: I think that we should all give an opinion and then I suggest that we vote.

B: Well, I would like to go to Argentina. I think the lake sounds fantastic.

C: Do you really? I would prefer to do something a bit more exciting. The Russian plane sounds incredible.

D: Yes, well, perhaps that's a little *too* exciting! I'd rather go somewhere with beautiful views, like the lake …

A: So, shall we vote on it? …

B: May I make a suggestion?

A: Yes, of course.

B: I suggest that we eliminate the lake, because it came last, and vote again.

Presenter: **Theme 10: Nutrition and Health, More Truths and Myths**
Lesson 2: Speaking review (1)
B 2 Listen to the first part of the conversation and check your ideas.

Lucas: I've found this great quiz in a magazine.

Ali: Really. Which magazine?

Lucas: Just a magazine.

Ali: But what's it called?

Lucas: It doesn't matter what it's called.

Ali: Well, where did you get it?

Lucas: It's not important where I got it.

Ali: OK. What's it about?

Lucas: It's about exercise … you know, the truths and myths about exercise.

Presenter: **C 2 Listen to the second part of the conversation and check your ideas.**

Benny: Sounds good. Shall we do it together?

Lucas: Well, I can't do it again because I know all the answers.

Murat: OK. Why don't you be the chairperson, then?

Lucas: All right. How shall we do the quiz? Individually? In teams?

Murat: You decide. You're the chairperson.

Lucas: No, it doesn't work like that. A chairperson makes sure everybody speaks and then, perhaps, conducts a vote.

Murat: OK. So, I think we should do the quiz in teams.

Lucas: That's a good idea. What do you think, Benny?

Benny: I'd rather do it individually.

Ali: That's because you're studying sports science. You'll know all the answers!

Benny: No. We haven't even *looked* at exercise yet on the course. It's all been about bones and muscles and the digestive system.

Murat: What's the significance of the digestive system in sports science?

Benny: Oh, come on, Murat. You are what you eat. Sports people have to eat exactly the right things to be fit.

Ali: What does *fit* mean?

Benny: You know. Able to run or walk for some time without getting out of breath.

Ali: Ah, right. So I am very *non*fit.

Benny: *Unfit.*

Ali: OK. Unfit. I'm very unfit.

Lucas: Can we get back to the quiz?

Murat: I'd prefer to work in teams … and I want to be on Benny's team.

Lucas: We haven't heard from you yet, Carlos.

Carlos: I'd like to work in teams, too. I think it's more fun.

Lucas: OK. Let's take a vote on it. Hands up all those in favour of teams. And those against. OK. That's three in favour and one against. Benny. Do you mind working in teams?

Murat: In my team.

Benny: No, that's fine.

Presenter: **D Listen to the third part, then explain.**

Lucas: OK. So two teams: Benny and Murat, Ali and Carlos. I will say each sentence and you have to decide if it's true or false. I think each team should discuss it and write T or F, then both teams should show me their choice.

All: OK. No problem. Fine.

Lucas: I won't tell you if you are right or wrong until the end.

Murat: Oh, no. We want to know straight away …

Ali: No, I think Lucas is right.

Presenter: **E Listen to the fourth part of the conversation and check your ideas.**

Lucas: OK. Statement 1. Exercise burns a lot of calories.

Murat: Well, of course that's true.

Lucas: Discuss it, then write down your choice. Don't let the other team hear you.
… OK. Team 1.

Murat: True.

Lucas: Team 2.

Ali: True. Are they all as easy as that?

Lucas: Statement 2. New-style exercise types like T'ai Chi, Pilates and Yoga are just silly.

Murat: I've never heard of them.

Ali: So *you're* silly.

Carlos: T'ai Chi comes from China, doesn't it?

Lucas: That's right.

Carlos: And yoga is from India, isn't it?

Lucas: Yes.

Carlos: But I haven't heard of Pilates.

Benny: I have. Pilates was a German gymnast, wasn't he? He treated himself for a serious neck problem and went on to treat other people.

Murat: And you said you haven't studied exercise yet!

Benny: I haven't! I read the college fitness club brochure.